FAITH IN POLITICS?

SARUM THEOLOGICAL LECTURES

FAITH IN POLITICS?

Rediscovering the Christian Roots of our Political Values

Richard Harries

DARTON · LONGMAN + TODD

First published in 2010 by
Darton, Longman and Todd Ltd
1 Spencer Court
140 – 142 Wandsworth High Street
London SW18 4JJ

ISBN 978-0-232-52787-2

A catalogue records for this book is available from the British Library.

Phototypeset by Kerrypress Ltd, Luton, Bedfordshire.
Printed and bound in Great Britain by Thomson Litho, East Kilbride, Scotland.

For Toby

CONTENTS

INTRODUCTION

The revelation in 2009 of the extent and nature of expenses claimed by MPs aroused almost universal feelings of outrage and derision. This was in some ways unfair, for all MPs were smeared, while some were shown to be exemplary in their claims. Moreover, the assumption behind the whole system of expense claims was wrong, and for this successive governments and the electorate as a whole must take some responsibility. Nevertheless, this scandal has had the effect of lowering the respect in which parliamentarians are held even further. Opinion polls regularly indicate that members of Parliament come very far down the list of those whom members of the public respect and trust. One of the latest polls on which professions are most trusted to tell the truth, or assumed to be lying, revealed that only 21 per cent of those polled trusted politicians to tell the truth. This was higher than journalists but shockingly low compared to the 92 per cent of those polled who trusted their doctor to be honest with them. This is not a situation about which we should simply shrug our shoulders and say, 'That's how it is.' It is unhealthy and potentially dangerous for our national life.

No doubt there has always been a fair degree of scepticism about politicians and their alleged altruism. Dr Johnson remarked that it was difficult to find a politician who was not on the make. As he told Boswell, 'politics are now nothing more than means of success in life.' Nevertheless, there have been those in all parties who were inspired to work for them, in some cases give their whole life for them, for altruistic as well as personal motives. For many, the Labour Party was a moral crusade to change society for the better on behalf of the poor. Within the Conservative Party there was a strong tradition of *noblesse oblige*.[1] Within the Liberal Party there were those who were driven by the need to bring about progressive social change. The vestiges of these attitudes are still there. Nevertheless, the general public believes that on the whole politicians are in it for themselves.

This distrust of politicians in general is also focused on governments. Only 29 per cent of British people trust their government, compared to the 66 per cent of the Dutch who trust theirs. The British figure is even lower than the European average of 34 per cent.

No doubt the media does not help. It likes to focus on the greasy-pole side of politics – who is climbing up and who is slipping down. Politicians continually urge that politics is about policies, and it should not be personalised in this way, and there is some justice in their complaint. Yet such is the distrust that the general public find it hard to go beyond questions of who is in and who is out of the ruling cabal. At the same time there is a profound mistrust of politics emanating from the media. Jeremy Paxman, so the caricature suggests, has only two questions: who are you and why are you lying to me?

In the light of this, it is not surprising that membership of all political parties has declined so rapidly. The media loves to focus on the alleged decline in attendance at church. What it ignores is that the decline in membership of political parties is far more dramatic. Membership of the Conservative Party has declined from 3 million members in the 1950s to less than 300,000, with a similar decline for Labour, whilst Liberal Democrat membership stands at just 60,000.

This suspicion and indifference is unhealthy. It undermines our public life and is potentially dangerous for society as a whole. And it concerns us all. Politics is too important to be left to politicians.

However, the situation is even more serious than this scepticism about individual politicians might suggest. People have become either cynical about or indifferent to the whole political system under which we live. The turn-out for elections is abysmal. Many of us will remember the huge queues in South Africa for the first election after the end of Apartheid. People had to queue for hours and in some cases days in order to cast their votes. By contrast, the people voting in the last general election constituted only 61.4 per cent of the electorate. This contrasts with the 83.9 per cent who turned out in 1950. Voting figures at other elections are even worse. Turn-out in Britain for European elections is usually around 35 per cent, but has fallen as low as 24 per cent. In local government elections the turn-out in 2006 in England was 36.5 per cent, and it has been lower. The situation amongst young people is even more disheartening. A Hansard Society survey in 2009 found that only 30 per cent of 18–24-year-olds had discussed politics or political news with someone else in the previous two or three years, compared with 47 per cent of their parents' generation.

There are a number of reasons for this low turn-out, not all of them sinister. One of them is that there is less difference in policies between the major political parties than there has sometimes been. There is a broad consensus on certain fundamental issues, and this, reflecting as it does a broad consensus in the electorate, ensures a certain stability, which is no bad thing.

Another reason is that our personal concerns are immediate and obvious, whereas political policies and systems can seem remote and not of very pressing import. However, political policies do make a difference to our personal lives. When a family member is ill we realise the importance of having a good National Health Service. If someone we know is suddenly made redundant, we recognise the importance of having a national economy that is prospering, as well as adequate safeguards for those who find themselves unemployed. The fact is that political policies vitally affect our lives, for good and ill.

Undergirding both policies and the process by which they are made is our political system and the values which it enshrines. Here, potentially, there is an even more serious malaise than lack of respect for politicians or indifference to political policies. It poses questions about whether our political system really matters and about the values from which it springs and which it embeds. Is this really a matter of indifference? Here we come to the heart of what this book is about. It is not about the various practical steps that might be taken to increase people's interest in politics, such as new electoral systems, more devolution of power to local councils and the whole field of constitutional reform. These are important subjects, but not the focus of this book, which is about the bedrock of the system itself.

This book is written in the conviction that the kind of political institutions, ideas and values that we enjoy today, which we either take for granted, or regard with a degree of scepticism, do matter very much. Furthermore, although it is widely held that the leading political notions of our time nearly all derive from European thinkers from the seventeenth to the nineteenth centuries, usually termed 'the Enlightenment', I will argue that these notions are in fact deeply embedded in a Christian understanding of what it is to be a human being in society. I have no desire at all to knock the Enlightenment, as has become fashionable in some theological circles. We are all heirs of the Enlightenment in one way or another, and glad to be so, not least when we read about some barbaric custom that still prevails in another country. But it is important to recognise that many of the leading Enlightenment thinkers regarded themselves as Christians, if of varying degrees of orthodoxy. Furthermore, the Enlightenment itself arose in and out of Christian soil, drawing on certain fundamental principles within it. I do not deny that in some respects Enlightenment principles had to be asserted against the hold of religious ortho-doxy, most notably in the case of religious liberty. It is fundamental to the Enlightenment that people must be left free to choose their religion, or reject it altogether, and this came hard to established religions, Catholic and Protestant, that were used to having a stranglehold on what people believed and practised. But as many Christians, such as John Locke, saw, religious liberty is fundamen-tal to genuine Christian faith. But this apart, in many other areas of thought that are considered in this book, the underlying Christian contribution is fundamental. In short, it is a book about rediscovering the Christian roots of our political values. These values are not exclusively Christian, and they are not asserted as being in principle hostile to Enlightenment ones, with which in some respects they may be identical. But our history and culture is a predominantly Christian one. Most people still claim to be Christians, whatever they mean by it. And it is important to tease out the fact that the political values which shape our society, and which are vital to our life together, are rooted in a particular understanding of what it is to be a human being in society. This is not just a matter of historical influence, though it is certainly that. Whether we approve of it or not, some of our most cherished values have come to us because our history has been shaped by the Christian faith. But it is more than a question of historical influence. The Christian understanding of what it is to be a human being in society has an abiding validity.

Anthony Seldon, writing on the lack of trust in our society and how it might be recovered, recounts the many indications of this lack of confidence in politics and politicians and then writes that it must be put in historical perspective:

> There is not the widespread lack of trust in British parties and the system of government that there was in the 1960's and 1970's, the late 1920's and the early 30's in Britain or in the inter-war years in Germany. For all the groans and screeching of the plates of the British body politics, no one is seriously advocating junking the entire system.[2]

They may not want to abandon the whole system but it is not in a healthy state.

Most people take our political values for granted. But from time to time a society is confronted by a crisis in which it is forced to ask in a serious way whether in fact it stands for anything at all. This country was faced by such a crisis in 1938. About that T. S. Eliot wrote at the time:

> I believe that there must be many persons who, like myself, were deeply shaken by the events of September 1938, in a

way from which one does not recover; persons to whom that month brought a profounder realization of a general plight ... It was not a criticism of the government, but a doubt of the validity of a civilization. We could not match conviction with conviction ... Was our society, which had always been so assured of its superiority and rectitude, so confident of its unexamined premises, assembled around anything more permanent than a congeries of banks, insurance companies and industries, and had it any beliefs more essential than a belief in compound interest and the maintenance of dividends?[3]

I do not believe we are faced by a comparably serious crisis now. International terrorism is very serious indeed, but it is not at the moment of the same order as the Nazi threat to Europe. But unless we take stock from time to time, and reaffirm the values by which we live, a crisis, if it comes, will find us wanting – as T. S. Eliot thought the Munich agreement found Britain wanting.

The first chapter of this book, on 'Speaking for God in a Secular Age', examines the basis on which the Church might claim to speak in and to the political arena. Although it is concerned significantly with its locus when commenting on political policies, it also includes the wider issue of the whole system and its values, in which those policies are decided and promulgated.

The second chapter, on 'Law and Morality', considers the basis of law, and argues that it has both a moral and a theological foundation. Law is a far less fashionable subject than democracy, for example, but it is in fact more fundamental to our way of life than even Parliament. Wise commentators rightly remarked that one of the many mistakes made in Iraq was the idea that democracy consisted mainly of getting an electoral system going, whereas in fact the rule of law is even more fundamental. Law is rooted in morality, and understanding what is the correct relationship between the two is vital to the health of a democracy. That relationship has changed in recent years, but it does not mean there is no relationship. That relationship remains vital for all areas of our political life.

The third chapter, on 'What Makes Us Think God Wants Democracy?', has a deliberately sceptical title because it is so easy simply to claim that a particular political system has religious backing, as was done for so long by advocates of the divine right of kings. But, aware of this, it is nevertheless maintained that 'Democracy is the worst system in the world – except for all the others.'[4] At the same time it is argued that it is above all a Christian understanding of what it is to be a human being in society that enables us to see the importance of democracy in its totality, both as an expression of a desire to live well together, and as a check on our tendency to pursue our own interests at the expense of others.

The fourth chapter, on 'Liberty, Equality and Human Community', looks at the three political values enshrined in the slogan of the French Revolution and argues that all three are absolutely fundamental to the Christian faith, and although they may be and are championed by a whole range of political philosophers, the Christian faith offers a sure grounding for them, which others may not share, but at least can recognise as such.

The fifth chapter, on 'Does God Believe in Human Rights?', again has a sceptical tone to it because a cursory reading of some parts of the Bible might give one the impression that he doesn't. Further, in some periods of its history the Church has in fact been an opponent of the rights which we now take for granted. Nevertheless, it is maintained that, properly understood, the Christian faith again offers a sure foundation for rights, and it is no accident that the prime movers to bring the UN Declaration on Human Rights into existence after World War II were some significant individual Christians.

The final chapter, on 'Who Do We Think We Are?', discusses questions of identity, which are crucial to understanding the world in which we live today. There is a very close connection between identity and religion, and this is the major reason why religion is such a potent factor in the world. The Christian faith offers some distinctive insights about the issue of identity, casting light on the question of who we think we are, which has implications for one of the major political concerns of our time.

There are some signs that the tectonic plates of the underlying political philosophy of our time are beginning to shift. One sign of this in 2009 was the publication of two major books on justice which challenge the received norms. One was by the Nobel prize winner Amartya Sen and the other was by the Reith Lecturer, Michael Sandel. Themes from both books are taken up in these chapters, for whilst they are both written from the standpoint of secular political philosophy, they are extraordinarily supportive of a Christian understanding of what it means to be a Christian in society. In particular, both books raise questions about 'the common good' and the need to work together to find some consensus on this. To this debate the Christian faith has much to contribute.

Some of the themes in this book have had a public outing before, for example in the Morrell Lecture in the University of York, in the David Nicholls Lecture in Oxford, at a seminar in the Faculty of Theology at Edinburgh University and, above all, in the Sarum Lectures, jointly sponsored by Salisbury Cathedral and Sarum College, to whom I am particularly grateful for the opportunity to shape up two-thirds of this book. The themes in this book are also those of my Gresham Lectures in the year 2009/10, whose audiences I thank for their attendance and questioning.

Richard Harries

SPEAKING FOR GOD IN A SECULAR AGE

THE CHANGING CONTEXT

The relationship between Christianity and the public realm is a highly controversial subject, about which people are highly suspicious and on which they have strong opinions. I understand those suspicions. If someone says, 'Christ came to save humanity', you may have difficulty making sense of it, or you may disagree with it, but you would recognise it as a Christian statement; a proclamation that you rightly expect the Church to make. If a Church leader says, 'Trident should not be replaced', you may agree with it, but you might understandably not regard it as a distinctively Christian position. It might be held by people with a range of religious and non-religious perspectives on life. So the suspicion is that if a Church leader pronounces on some aspect of public life, it might be just his personal view, or the view of a particular section of society; and you wonder whether there is any integral connection between the policy so advocated and the Christian faith.

The late Enoch Powell, who was converted to the Christian faith from atheism as an adult, and who was a serious biblical scholar, put the issue starkly when he said that the teaching of Jesus was inward, individual and eschatological, and defeated every attempt to get a political policy from it. There is some truth in that view, which I will be considering later, and which is why we have the suspicion that I mentioned. Nevertheless, his conclusion is false. I hope to show that we can legitimately try to achieve a public policy that has an integral connection to the Christian faith, albeit on particular issues there will still sometimes be scope for some disagreement.

For nearly three centuries the Church was a small, spasmodically persecuted sect in the Roman Empire. Its main concern was the quality of its own life, both that of its individual members, and the face it presented corporately to the world. Nevertheless, it had to have some attitude to the political structures of the time, and the New Testament makes it clear what that was to be. Writing towards the end of the first century or the beginning of the second, the writer of the first letter to Timothy put it this way:

> First of all, then, I urge that petitions, prayers, intercessions, and thanksgivings be offered for everyone, for sovereigns and for all in high office so that we may lead a tranquil and quiet life, free to practice our religion with dignity.

> 1 Timothy 2:1–2

That could not be clearer. They simply wanted to be left alone so that they could worship God in peace and witness to the faith without being harassed. That has been the attitude of many Christians since, sometimes because the government has been hostile to the Church, as in the Soviet Union, and sometimes as a matter of Christian policy, as with sects like the Plymouth Brethren.

After the conversion of the Emperor Constantine to Christianity in the fourth century, the Church achieved a position of power, and its relationship to the state became very different – too close, many would say. Christianity became the official religion of the Empire, and Constantine was seen as God's vice-regent on earth. But for the purposes of my theme, I need to jump straight from there to the opening paragraph of A. J. P. Taylor's history of the first half of the twentieth century. There he wrote:

> Until August 1914, a sensible law abiding Englishman could pass through life and hardly notice the existence of the State, beyond the post office and policeman. All this was changed by the impact of the Great War.[1]

'All this was changed.' The state now dominates our lives in a way it did not before. In particular, the state has become the monopoly provider in areas where previously the Church had the major responsibility – education, social welfare and health.[2]

Speaking for God in a Secular Age

For most of the Church's history it was possible for Christians to show their love for their neighbour either by individual acts of kindness, or by getting together with others to found schools, hospitals, hospices, orphanages and so on. The witness of the Church in these fields down the ages has been impressive. But how can someone care about their neighbour today without being concerned about the public policies which affect so much of their lives, either for good or ill? Love of neighbour today has an inescapable political dimension. To think we can love our neighbours without being concerned about the political policies which shape their lives is to live in unreality.

That does not, of course, answer the question about what that love of neighbour entails in terms of political policies; it simply opens the question up. It also poses further questions about what the Church should say and how it should say it. But this presupposes a prior issue about the kind of society we now find ourselves in. People talk about living in a secular society or a secular age. The title of this chapter is 'Speaking for God in a Secular Age', so let me begin by trying to think as clearly as possible about the concept of the secular.

THE SECULAR

First we must distinguish between a 'secular age' and a 'secular society'. The first term is a description of the kind of society we live in. The second term is put forward as a model for the relationship our political structures should have to religion.

I will take the concept of a secular age first. In the 1960s it was argued by some that the West was in the process of an irreversible process of secularisation. Then people began to ask rather more critical questions about the kind of criteria that might be used to judge this. It was pointed out that France, for example, had some 40,000 professional fortune-tellers, which was more than the number of priests in the country; hardly a sign of a secular society. Since then there has been lively and often better-focused debate, with either the eighteenth century or the 1960s seen as the key period of change in the direction of secularisation.

Charles Taylor, in his book *A Secular Age*,[3] which won the Templeton Prize, contrasts life in 1500 with life today. In 1500 belief in God was the unquestioned assumption behind the whole of life, political and personal. Today that is no longer the case. Taylor does not believe that religious faith will become ever more marginal. What he says is that today the Christian faith is one option amongst others. Furthermore, at least in the circles where many Christians move, they have to argue for the truth of their faith against the prevailing *zeitgeist* which assumes the opposite. I recognise the description that Taylor gives, and believe that it is an accurate one of the kind of society in which we now live. It is important to note that Taylor does not think Christianity untrue – indeed, he himself is a believer – nor does he think it will die out, but we do live in a secular age, in his sense of the term, compared with, for example, the year 1500. Our fundamental assumptions as a society have shifted. Our age is one in which the Christian faith is one option amongst others, and in many circles, perhaps most, it has to be argued for against the prevailing intellectual assumptions. This is what I mean by living in a secular age.

The term 'secular society' is no less contentious. It refers to a set of institutional arrangements for a shared public and social life. From this point of view, therefore, a secular society is not so much a description of what prevails in some countries, but a project which people support or oppose. It is not about belief, for it is totally compatible to be a Christian believer and support a secular society. However, we can note a link here between the description of a secular age and the project for a secular society, in the sense that support for a secular society first emerged when people began to see themselves as living in a secular age. First, however, we have to tease out what might actually be meant by a 'secular society', for this too is contentious. France claims to be a secular society, but the state pays for the upkeep of church buildings. England is not a secular society, for we have an established Church, but the Church itself has to pay for the upkeep of its buildings. So it is not obvious what the term 'secular society' might involve.

My starting point is the position of the distinguished scholar Amartya Sen, and his discussion of India.[4] Sen argues that a secular society is one in which the state treats all religions equally. The relationship between the state and its religions may be close or distant; that does not matter. The point is that in a secular state, which he regards as desirable, they are all treated equally. He believes that India is in principle such a state. In India, as we know, religion is a fundamental feature of human existence. He argues that the Indian constitution allows all religions to participate in public life on an equal basis, though of course, as we know, that position is highly contested by some Hindu nationalists, notably the Bharatiya Janata Party (BJP), who argue that India is a Hindu country and this should be reflected in its political life and structures. A good example of a policy which follows Amartya Sen's principle in our own country is that of state funding of faith schools. All the major faiths can qualify for state funding of their faith-based schools on an equal basis. So this is an example of a close relationship between the state and religion, but on Sen's definition it still fits the idea of a secular society in that it is based on the principle that all religions are treated equally.

A rather different point of view is argued by Ronald Dworkin in relation to the United States of America.[5] The First Amendment of the American constitution makes a clear separation between the state and religion. However, in recent years there have been vigorous advocates of the position which says that because America is predominantly a Christian believing country, this should, for example, be reflected by prayers in state schools, which are forbidden at the moment. All are agreed that religious tolerance is fundamental. The issue is between a minimal religious state in which religion is in certain respects privileged, and a minimal secular state where it is kept out of public institutional arrangements altogether. Dworkin argues strongly for the latter. In short, he does not just say, as does Sen, that all religions should be treated on an equal basis. He maintains that they should be equally excluded from all public structures and institutions.

Here I must raise, however briefly, the question of establishment. Leaving aside Dworkin's view for the moment, and supposing you are sympathetic to that of Amartya Sen, of treating all religions equally, on what possible basis can you justify privileging one religion over another, particularly if we live in a secular age, in which Christianity has to argue its case, often against the prevailing opinion that it is not true and might even be harmful?

Here I would want to suggest that we cannot ignore the history and culture of a society, which will inevitably be reflected in its political arrangements, and the religion of a society is an integral part of that history and culture, part of its identity. We are not just isolated individuals. Our membership of families, communities and society is a fundamental feature of our identity. It is therefore legitimate to take the history, culture and religion of our society into account when we are thinking of our political arrangements. However, we need to make a distinction between what is a purely symbolic privilege, and one in which other religions feel that their rights are being denied. There can be no question of privileging one religion in a way that denies fundamental human rights to others. However, when it comes to symbolic privilege, then it seems to me a matter of courtesy and negotiation as to whether these should remain. This is a big subject which it is not possible to pursue now, except to say that it is paradoxical that the strongest defenders of the establishment of the Church of England at the moment tend to be Jewish and Muslim leaders. They argue that having an established church helps them make their own contribution to public life. In short, using my distinction, they clearly do not feel that their rights are in any way compromised, and they accept a degree of symbolic privilege for a religion other than their own. Clearly that latter position must always be open to change and negotiation. For it is easy for the dominant religion to think that it is tolerant when others in fact experience it as oppressive.[6]

Putting the question of establishment aside, I now return to Dworkin's view about keeping religion completely out of all politically structured public space. But this can mean two things. It can mean not having prayer in state schools. And it can go beyond this to say that religious bodies should not be trying to influence public policy at all on the basis of their religion. Here Rowan Williams has made a useful distinction, now widely shared by others, between a market-place from which religion has been excluded, and one in which there is a multiplicity of voices, including those of religious bodies. Behind these two attitudes we can discern two rather different approaches by thinkers of the Enlightenment: that of Locke on the one hand and that of Voltaire on the other. Locke wanted a society which was free for religion – all religions. This is what we have in America. Voltaire wanted a society which was free from religion. This is what we have, at least in part, in France. In fact, whether we like it or not, in a democratic society we are bound to have a crowded market-place in which religious voices, amongst others, will be seeking to be heard, and trying to persuade others that certain political policies are better than others. That is very obviously the case in the United States, where advocates of religiously based policies have been militant on such issues as abortion. Not all of these have been from a right-wing standpoint, though these gained most attention during the Bush administration. One of the interesting features of the Obama campaign for President was his attempt to win back the association of religion and politics from the right to more progressive policies. This is of the greatest significance. Before then in America, it was the political right who were associated with trying to bring religion into politics, whilst the left tended to adopt the view that religion is a personal affair, and in the political realm we should argue in secular terms. The significance of Obama's stance is that it is a sign that the progressive left is less content with that view, and wishes to argue for a religiously based, or at least morally based, view of the common good against the alternative that had prevailed under George Bush.

RELIGIOUS VOICES IN PUBLIC PLACES

We now live in a plural society, in which people have a range of views about the meaning and purpose of life, and from this different understandings of what makes for the good life and a

---

good society. Sometimes the disagreements between these views are radical and fierce, as in the so-called culture wars in America. It is important, therefore, in such a society, to try to find some basic principles on the basis of which we can participate in the political realm, whilst disagreeing on what has been termed our 'comprehensive views' or 'world-views'. The most important voice in recent years in trying to sketch out such principles is John Rawls, and fundamental to his position is that our comprehensive views, religious and otherwise, must be kept out of the picture when devising the basic principles on the basis of which we will conduct out politics. His position is that we can bring our comprehensive views into the background culture but not into the body politic.

It is not always easy to understand what John Rawls's position implies in the first place, and he has altered his position somewhat over the years, with the result that he is variously interpreted. But most fundamentally, there is the question of whether an approach like his can succeed, and the further question about whether it is even desirable.[7]

My own view, on the key issues thrown up by Rawls are, first, that despite his disclaimer, what he advocates is in itself a comprehensive view, one which gives overriding value to the principles of religious freedom and equal treatment. Secondly, the concept of public reasoning remains a rather vague term, but properly understood does not exclude the contribution of a religious perspective to public political debate, even when it is not translated out of religious terms into a form of rational secular argument. Thirdly, it is not really possible to draw a sharp line between background culture and the body politic.

In short, for a pluralistic liberal democracy to remain stable, religions must find reasons from within their own perspective to accept the basic political institutions which express and safeguard the values of personal liberty, especially where religion is concerned, and equal treatment. I agree with Nicholas Wolterstorff, who writes:

the state must not differentiate in its treatment of citizens on account of their religion or lack thereof, and there must be no differentiation among citizens in their right to voice in the conduct and personnel of the state on account of their religion or lack thereof.[8]

He argues that the stability of a society depends on religions, from their own perspective, accepting these principles of organisation, rather than on Rawls's view that they need to have reasons from their own perspective for appealing to public reason. The two principles he outlines as fundamental are freedom of religion, and equal treatment of peoples, in my view, part of a comprehensive doctrine, one which in fact lies behind the attempt by Rawls to devise a basis for a political life independent of any such view.

As the discussion of Rawls can become very abstract, I would like to draw on my own experience to illuminate what might or might not be implied by some of the key terms in this debate, and how it is that a religious perspective can make its contribution.

In the debates on stem cell research a key question is of course the moral status of the early embryo. So the issue cannot be discussed without taking into account people's comprehensive world-view. Some think we are dealing at this stage – that is, before fourteen days – simply with a bundle of multiplying cells smaller than a pin-head. Others – Roman Catholics, for example – believe that what we have here is due all the respect of a human person. It was inevitable and right that they should bring that perspective into the debate. In my own contributions in the House of Lords I tried to show that the Christian tradition was not as monolithic as Roman Catholics suggest, and that until 1869 a distinction was made in the moral seriousness of abortion depending on whether it was early or late, and this reflected a more gradualist understanding of the status of the foetus. The point here is not who is right or wrong on these issues but the inevitability and rightness of bringing a religious perspective into the discussion. A few years ago, when the then Chief Rabbi, Lord Jakobovits, an expert on Jewish medical ethics, was in the Lords, his contribution in this field from that perspective was valued. This debate on stem cell research was a process of public reasoning, in that although people deeply disagreed with one another, it was conducted in a courteous manner, speakers understood one another and did not resent the fact that others drew their views from different religious and moral traditions.

It is also important to note that the concept of public reasoning is not as neutral as it might at first sight seem. In recent debates in the House of Lords on assisted dying, there was almost no appeal to a specifically religious argument. On the other hand, it was clear that the weighting given to certain arguments did often depend on a person's underlying philosophical and religious perspective on life. This point is also made by Jonathan Chaplin in a recent *Theos* booklet.[9]

In the debates on stem cell research it was neither possible nor desirable for the religious basis of different positions to be translated into non-religious terms. A different situation was present in the debates on assisted dying. Although secularists fiercely accused the religious of blocking legislation to allow assisted dying, the debate was in fact conducted, as already mentioned, with almost no reference to religion. It was all in terms of what would be the effect of a law allowing assisted dying, the nature of suffering, the dignity of human beings and what it means to be a human being. In fact, of course, a religious perspective colours and shapes the answer to these questions about suffering, dignity and what it is to be a human being, but in this debate the religious base did not have to be spelt out. This is because although much religious belief in the past has been put in terms of what God commands or what he wills, what God commands is designed for our common good, and we can translate a religious imperative into a discussion about what makes for the common good when it is appropriate to do so. Furthermore, Christianity is not only about God, it is about what it is for human beings to be made in the image of God. So a religious perspective can here also be easily translated into a discussion about the proper way to value human beings. All this is expressed in the traditional Christian doctrine of natural law,

Speaking for God in a Secular Age

whose assumption is that people of different religious views and none can come together on certain agreed moral values, and a shared understanding of the public goods which all societies need.

The other aspect we need to bear in mind is that there are cultural differences between different societies, and an appeal to religion may be natural in one society but not in another. The obvious example of this, of course, is the contrast between the United States and Britain. Because of its history, America has the paradox of a constitution which is religiously neutral, but a public sphere in which the religious dimension is a major feature. In Britain just the opposite is true, for we have an established Church but people feel very uncomfortable about people claiming the high moral ground through an appeal to religion. So on the one hand, almost every American politician will make some reference to God in their public utterances, but Tony Blair kept religious references out of his speeches on the grounds, as he said afterwards, that he did not want to be dismissed as 'a nutter'.

That said, whilst for many normal purposes it might be natural to use public reasoning, the language of common discourse without appeal to religious foundations or motivations, there may very well be occasions when a more prophetic voice is needed, and one in which the Christian dimension is made clear. I do not think this is an issue on which Christians should divide. It is partly a matter of temperament. More importantly, it is a matter of judgement, bearing in mind the culture, the issue and the audience.

This highlights an obvious point about such debates today. If the appeal is simply to a religious authority, whether it is the Bible, the Qur'an or any other sacred book, it will be persuasive only to some, and will have the effect of alienating others. So in that sense it is not sensible or effective to use a direct appeal to religious authority. But my point is that in some debates, as for example over stem cell research or abortion, we cannot avoid bringing in fundamentally divergent religious and non-religious views, and in other debates such as assisted dying, a theological perspective translates very easily into non-religious terms, though it might be better to say that a theological perspective gives a particular colour to non-religious concepts and arguments whilst itself remaining hidden. People too often assume that a religious perspective offers a straightforward alternative to a non-religious one. In fact the way that a religious perspective best operates is by illuminating some field of which naturally we are only dimly aware. It helps us to see truths that may be half hidden. As an example I would point to the work of Reinhold Niebuhr and how his Christian understanding of man, with our capacity for justice and our inclination to injustice, brought such illumination to the study of politics, both national and international, that he was hugely influential in secular departments of politics and international affairs, as well as on front-rank politicians on these subjects over two decades.[10]

The implications of this seem to me that, first, a liberal democracy does imply a particular world-view, and for religions to be part of it, and make their contribution to its political ordering and policies, they have to accept the institutions which express and preserve the principles of freedom of religion and equal treatment. This means that those who advocate violence cannot be part of it, nor those whose views are overtly racist, for example. Such people will be excluded, and here we have to face the fact that a liberal democratic society, like every other, depends on a degree of coercion. Those who incite violence will be arrested, charged, and if found guilty, imprisoned.

With that vitally important proviso, it does not seem to me that this excludes the propagation of views that might be radically different and even alien to the prevailing culture. I see no reason, for example, why Muslims, if they wanted to, could not campaign for the right to have more than one wife. They might even translate their argument into a discussion of what might be good for society, rather than simply drawing on the authority of the Qur'an or Muslim tradition. They might be unwise to campaign for such a change, and they might not be very successful, but I see nothing in a liberal democratic polity which would prevent them from so doing. It is possible in theory that such a policy would gain widespread assent and be voted through Parliament.

The mention of marriage highlights another way in which the state does not remain neutral as far as comprehensive doctrines are concerned. If in fact the state was neutral, it would not legally sanction any particular form of relationship. People would be left free to enter into monogamous, androgynous or polygamous relationships as they chose. In fact in the UK, as in the USA, the law recognises only monogamy, defined as the union of one man with one woman to the exclusion of all others, for life. This is a Christian view of marriage. It is not neutral. Following on from this, it is possible to argue that the state should also recognise civil partnerships between people of the same sex because such partnerships reflect similar values to the ones it already recognises in marriage. In short, the argument for civil partnerships is not simply a libertarian one, that people should be free to choose their own lifestyle. It is that marriage exists for a particular purpose, and as such enshrines a particular understanding of what is good for society, and, by extension, a civil partnership can do the same.

The debate on these issues is not only of importance to Christians, but, of course, to Muslims. On the view taken here there is no reason why Muslims should not contribute to our political life, drawing quite explicitly on Islamic sources when they thought it was helpful and appropriate to do so. On other occasions, they may well find it is quite possible, as well as wise, to engage in a form of public reasoning where the religious foundation of the view is hidden and the language is more secular. However, there is a particular challenge to Muslims to accept the two fundamental assumptions of a liberal democracy – religious freedom and equal treatment. It is very heartening that a good number of Muslim thinkers today are drawing on Islamic tradition to do just that.

What this whole debate has brought to the fore is that we cannot escape the necessity of a continuing public debate about the nature of a good society. Libertarians have wanted to avoid this for very understandable reasons. First, the fierce disagreements about the nature of that good society which makes the prospect of a consensus remote, and secondly, the fear that bringing comprehensive doctrines into the political sphere could lead to the oppression or marginalisation of minority views by the majority whose view prevailed. However, as Michael Sandel has convincingly shown, secular philosophies, when pushed to their logical conclusion, find that they simply cannot avoid facing questions about the nature of the good and what makes for a good society. This is an issue which is followed up in the final chapter.

THE TEACHING OF JESUS AND PUBLIC POLICY

Now we need to look more closely at the reasons why Christianity should have a concern to influence public policy. I have indeed already suggested one reason. It is not possible to love our neighbour without considering the effect of political policies on her or him, because the state dominates so much of our lives. But there is another no less fundamental one.

At the heart of the teaching of Jesus was his proclamation of the Kingdom of God. Mark's Gospel begins with his call that people should *metanoia* – that is, re-think their lives – and put themselves under the kingship of God, whose Kingdom Jesus was ushering in.

Behind this lies the age-old hope of the Jewish people that God would decisively act to put right everything that has gone wrong in this world, and establish his just and gentle rule. This is a hope for the whole of human life. In the Hebrew Scriptures religion concerns every aspect of the community – economic, legal, political. With the coming of the Kingdom, life in its every aspect, personal and political, inward and outward, was to be transformed. So although Enoch Powell, to take him as representing a point of view, is right to suggest that Jesus addressed people as individuals, and he first of all appealed to their inward dimension, their heart and mind, the Kingdom into which he invited them concerns the totality of life.

Powell, however, pointed to three aspects of the teaching of Jesus which he thought made it impossible to get a political programme from it. It is not only addressed to individuals, appealing to their hearts and minds. It is eschatological. And here is a real difficulty, one with which the Church has struggled in every age. To put it briefly, those whom Jesus called put themselves under God's rule, and by doing so in some sense entered his Kingdom, but he seemed to suggest that this Kingdom was to come in its fullness very soon. But did it? Jews say, 'No. Life goes on much as it did before. There has been no Messianic age.' 'Yes', say the Christians, 'for in some decisive sense it has come in the death and resurrection of Jesus, the beginning of the end. In him evil and death are over-thrown, as they are overthrown for all who put their trust in him. But,' say the Christians, 'the end is yet to come. We live between the times, between Christ's rising and his coming again in glory, when the Kingdom comes in its full consummation.' The importance of this for Christian theology and ethics cannot be exaggerated, nor the challenge it has offered the Church in every age. We see Christians in the New Testament having to adjust to the fact that the coming again of Christ in glory was not as soon as they first thought. By the end of the New Testament period they are having to adjust to the reality that the Church may be a continuing institution in a world that might go on for quite some time yet.

This delay in the *parousia* posed, and continues to pose, a number of questions which concern the whole area of Christian ethics and Christian lifestyles.[11] However, from the point of view of my theme here, there is one major question. Does the teaching of Jesus apply just to our personal relationships, or is it meant to apply as well to our public role? For example, Jesus said:

> Do not resist those who wrong you. If anyone slaps you on the right cheek, turn and offer him the other also. If anyone wants to sue you and takes your shirt, let him have your cloak as well. If someone in authority presses you into service for one mile, go with him two. Give to anyone who asks; and do not turn your back on anyone who wants to borrow.

> Matthew 5:39–42

Yet towards the end of the third century we find Christians beginning to join the army. Were they right to do so? In the fifth century St Augustine acted as a magistrate, meting out the tough punishments that were usual in the Roman Empire. Was he right to do so? A number of Chancellors of the Exchequer have been believing Christians, as have bankers. Should they have given to anyone who asked them for money?

It is important to note that this tension is not just between our private life and our public role. It is also present in our private life, and in the life of the Church itself, for the fact of the matter is that for most of our decisions, we act on the assumption that we need to plan responsibly for the future. We take out insurance, for example, and religious communities build up endowments, whereas Jesus is recorded as saying that we are not to be anxious about the future. We are to set our mind on God's Kingdom and his justice before everything else, trusting that our needs will be looked after (Matt. 6:33). However, the sharpest tension, the one with which I am concerned, is that between what we might do in a personal capacity and what we usually regard as our responsibility in a public role.

A familiar position is that of St Augustine, who took the view that whilst Christians belong to the City of God, which is being built up in human history, so long as that history lasts we have to co-operate with others to help ensure the basic goods of life such as order and a minimal justice, without which no human society can exist. We have to work with others for the commonalities of life, those essentials that we share with everyone. This meant for someone like Luther that, whilst God rules the world through love expressed in our personal relationships, he also rules the world through the coercion exercised by the state. So he thought that if he was attacked when preaching the Gospel, he should not resist, but if he was attacked as a citizen, he had a duty as a citizen to do so. In fact, for most of Christian history, this kind of dualism, in one form or another, has been the norm.

Some Christians have taken a totally contrary position and argued that the clear implications of the teaching of Jesus cannot

Speaking for God in a Secular Age

be evaded, and Christians should not take part in public life. They refuse to join the army. Sometimes they disassociate themselves as far as they can from all involvement with wider society, the best-known example at the moment being the Mennonite communities in the United States. There are also some influential and well-respected theologians who similarly suggest that the job of the Church is to be the Church, enacting the full range of the demands of Jesus without qualification or evasion, but that in no way should we get involved with the political structures and policies of the world on their terms, for this involves illegitimate compromises.[12] We can and must witness to the world, but only on our terms, with our radical message.

Here is a very clear example of that position by two American authors:

> We do not believe God has a double ethic. We do not believe God ordains a higher ethic for especially devout folk and a lower ethic for the masses. We do not believe that God intends Christians to wait until the millennium to obey the Sermon on the Mount. We do not believe God commands one thing for the individual and another for that same person as a public official.[13]

I believe that both the positions that I have mentioned are unsatisfactory. The first one, represented by Augustine and Luther, is indeed too dualistic. The second one, in rejecting all dualism, fails to grasp the implications of living between the times. For as long as God wills human life to continue to exist, he wills human communities and societies to exist, for as Austin Farrer put it, 'mind is a social reality'. We are essentially, not just contingently, inter-personal. We would not exist as persons without other persons who have talked us into talking and then into that interior talking that we call thinking. But human societies, certainly above a certain size, cannot exist without a degree of coercion, even if it is only the bobby on the beat with the law behind him. It may not have been so in Eden, but it is now, and therefore so long as God wills human life to continue, he wills human communities to continue with an element of coercion without which they cannot hold together. We could also make a rather different kind of argument for saying that so long as we live on this earth, responsible planning for the future is a moral imperative. We rightly think about things like pensions so that we might not be a burden on others. We should take thought for the morrow, even if, as Jesus said, we should not be obsessively anxious about it.

But this should not lead to a total dualism. For the radical imperative of Jesus does bear upon public policy because the Kingdom he came to proclaim and inaugurate concerns the whole of human life, all that makes for human well-being and flourishing. The Divine Rule bears upon outward life as well as inward, material and well as spiritual, economic, political and social as well as inter-personal. However, so long as we continue on this earth, that imperative cannot be responded to as though it was the only consideration. It lives in tension with the practical, prudential considerations that we have to take into account if we are going to have any kind of responsible, ordered existence. It lives in tension in two ways. In living before the absolute ideal of the Kingdom, we are aware always of a falling short. It may be the best we can do in the circumstances, but it is not what will finally prevail in the *milieu* of divine glory. Secondly, and this is the key point, that absolute ideal beckons us to approximate to it, so far as we can in the circumstances of a finite, fallen world. We are not simply to resign ourselves to a brutal realism. We are not simply to shrug our shoulders and say that nothing can be changed.

Let me take the example of the criminal justice system. Jesus said we are to forgive up to seventy times seven – that is, without limit. Tolstoy believed that society, not just individuals, should live by this principle. The police, the courts, prisons: all should be abolished. Most people take a more realistic view. They believe that if that happened, anarchy would ensue and human life as we know it would become impossible. The position for which I am arguing agrees that we need the criminal justice system. But it does not rest content with that. It says that the imperative of Jesus still bears upon it and we need to explore ways in which it can make a difference. An obvious one, of course, is that we are never to lose sight of the fact that people in prison are human beings like ourselves, created by God and redeemed by Christ, and we must work for their rehabilitation into society and growth into the people whom God has it in mind for them to be. So prisons must never be simply places where people are locked up to punish them and keep them out of the way. They should be places in which their restoration to the community as good citizens is never lost sight of. Another potentially very creative development is restorative justice, originally pioneered by the Thames Valley Police and now taken up in a limited way elsewhere. This brings together the victim and the perpetrator of the crime. In short, the ethic of Jesus should act as a catalyst on public policy, motivating us to look for new possibilities of making it a reality, so far as we can in the world as we know it.

WHAT WE ASK OF THE STATE

Earlier I quoted a sentence by A. J. P. Taylor about the role of the state in our lives: 'All this was changed by the impact of the Great War.' The state now dominates our lives in a way it did not do before. But there is another aspect of that change, which has to do with the changing conditions of our lives and our expectations about them. In the Fitzwilliam Museum in Cambridge there is a gloomy painting by Salvator Rosa (1615–73). Underneath are written the words, 'Conception is sinful, birth a punishment, life hard labour, death inevitable.' Samuel Beckett could not have done better. For most of human history life was very hard, and for the majority of people, very hard indeed. Nasty, brutish and short, as Thomas Hobbes put it. People had little expectation that it could be changed for the better, and they viewed life as a moral obstacle course which, if successfully surmounted, led to a better one afterwards. Take just one aspect, infant mortality, which was incredibly high even in the nineteenth century. Grieving parents could only just about cope with it on the basis of a strong faith that their infants would go to heaven.

Salvator Rosa painted his picture in the seventeenth century, but by the eighteenth century things were already beginning to change. People began to think that the conditions of human life ought to be improved, and with the industrial revolution, the development of scientific medicine, public health policies, and the ever more rapid advances in science and technology in the twentieth century, not least in the life sciences in recent decades, they could be improved. And that has proved to be the case in the West. So instead of looking to the state simply to maintain the status quo, to provide order and a minimum of justice, we now expect it to play its part in changing the conditions in which human beings live their lives.

St Paul saw the role of the state in terms of punishing wrongdoing (Rom. 13:1–6). We do not see the state only in these narrow terms. Governments, elected by the people, are there not only to judge but to order our common life for the common good. We have a conviction that, within limits, this can be done and ought to be done.[14]

In the nineteenth century, partly no doubt as a result of Darwin's theory of evolution, people began to think in terms of the inevitable advance of society and civilisation. Christians began to think of the gradual establishment of the Kingdom of God on earth. This easy optimism was shattered by the impact of World War I. But in any case, the idea of the gradual advance of the Kingdom of God on earth as reflected in improving social conditions is not a New Testament idea. However, the danger of reacting against ideas of automatic progress is that Christians could be lulled into thinking that the time between Christ's rising and his coming in glory is simply a time of waiting. But that again is untrue to the New Testament. The early Church believed that this in-between time displays signs of the Kingdom. The Church itself is one such sign, a pledge of the new society which has been recreated round Jesus. The early Church also recorded miracles, which it regarded as signs of the breaking in of the Kingdom of God.

I do not think we should necessarily look for miracles in terms of the old definition of events that are contrary to nature. But we should expect signs – signs that the reign of God has broken into this world in the death and resurrection of Jesus Christ, a reign which will come into its consummation in God's good time. Meanwhile we have the Holy Spirit working with and in and through us, bringing signs of that time when all things will be transformed. It is a mistake for Christians simply to wait for that end time. It is equally a mistake to talk about building up God's Kingdom on earth. It is not a mistake to try to let God work in and through us to bring some change that is at the same time an inkling of a better, utterly changed world. As a prayer by Percy Dearmer puts it:

> O God,
> who set before us the great hope
> that your kingdom shall come on earth
> and taught us to pray for its coming:
> give us grace to discern the signs of its dawning
> and to work for the perfect day
> when the whole world shall reflect your glory;
> through Jesus Christ our Lord.

Acting in the everyday world, including the political and economic spheres, to make a difference, with that difference perhaps indicating in some way the total difference of God's future, is how we bring the imperative of Jesus to bear upon the hard realities of the world as we know it. So long as we are in this world there will be an ineradicable tension between those hard realities and that imperative which impels us to something different. But that imperative stirs us to look for possibilities that may not be obvious to the hard-headed realist. For the possibilities are the possibilities of the God who has disclosed himself in the resurrection of Jesus from the dead. Those possibilities do not do away with the realities of the world, even whilst they may challenge our too-narrow understanding of what is possible. Reinhold Niebuhr used to describe the ethic of Jesus as 'An impossible possibility'. A critic of Niebuhr wrote a book entitled *The Relevance of the Impossible*, which is an equally useful phrase to indicate how the ethic of Jesus bears upon the world. It is relevant. It makes a difference even in the toughest world of politics. But it does not abolish that world, and it can be realised only in a proximate form.

CHRISTIAN FAITH AND PUBLIC POLICY – TWO EXAMPLES

A very dramatic example of the tension I am talking about occurred at the time of the Suez crisis in 1956. Archbishop Geoffrey Fisher was deeply suspicious about what was happening even at a time when he did not know about the collusion between Britain and Israel. In one dramatic debate in the House of Lords he intervened eight times with the same simple question: 'Who then was the attacker?' Lord Hailsham, who was defending the Government's position in the Lords, was furious, and he and Fisher had a long and politely ferocious exchange of letters.

What is most interesting is Fisher's serious intellectual grappling with the general question of what was appropriate for a Church leader to say in such circumstances. In one letter (of 11 closely typed pages of A5 paper)[15] he said that he and Hailsham had 'Quite different conceptions as to the principles which ought to guide an Archbishop in discharging his duties'.[16] His starting point is the duty of obedience to God. 'It is the ceaseless task of the Christian and the Christian minded state to strive after that one obedience.' There are two interesting points about that sentence. First, the reference simply to 'the Christian' – a reference that would include both Archbishop and lay person, and that lay person in both their private and their public roles. Secondly, the phrase 'Christian minded state'. It implies, in a rather careful way, that the state, as a state, is to strive after that one obedience. It is doubtful if now, what is so often referred to as our multi-faith society, would be receptive to this kind of language, but the Archbishop felt it was still appropriate in 1956.

So, there is 'one obedience', but the Archbishop then goes on to say that the Government, which of course Hailsham was representing, and he as Archbishop, approach this from opposite ends. The Government is concerned with the temporal ends of the society it governs, but he as Archbishop is concerned, referring to God, 'To relate what I can perceive of his perfect will to our temporal affairs ... that is my special contribution.' He said that, starting from different ends, it is not surprising that they do not come to an exact meeting point. When that is the case, 'It is our duty to call to each other so that we may help and warn each other.'

Fisher then quotes Temple to the effect that we can only look at issues properly if we can exorcise self-centredness, but interest-ingly, he applies this not to the individual case, but to public policy. A government will inevitably look at issues from a national perspective. He, as Archbishop, will look at them from a much wider view, and he reminds Hailsham, rather sharply, that he has duties not only to the nation, but to the wider world, and in particular to the wider Church at home and abroad. Which leads again to his emphasis on referring the matter to the UN as a way of approaching that wider perspective.

This letter is very revealing, and although Fisher is not usually rated as a theologian, it seems to me that his understanding of the respective roles of politician and Church leader, and how they might approach the issue, could hardly be bettered. What we note above all is that whilst there is a tension, there is no absolute dualism. There is a proper difference of roles, a genuine tension, but no abyss between the two.

I now come to the final aspect of this subject that I wish to consider. How specific should Church leaders be in trying to speak for God? It is possible to speak in very general terms. 'Both sides should strive for peace.' But this can be platitudinous and in fact amount to saying nothing. As David Jenkins used to say, 'Generally speaking bishops are generally speaking.' At the oppo-site extreme, a statement can be quite specific in advocating a particular policy. The disadvantage of this, of course, is that it will almost certainly be controversial, and raise questions as to how far the Church leader is speaking for the Church and not just himself or herself. Could Christians recognise it as a Christian statement, one which has an integral connection to the faith? This brings us back to a difficulty I raised right at the beginning.

There is much to be said for a position between these two extremes. This involves setting out Christian principles which should be taken into account whilst recognising that it is the statesman, not the churchman, who has to make the decision and bear responsibility for it. A good example of this is the set of criteria known as the Just War principles, which have been much to the fore in debates over the last 50 years, first in relation to the nuclear issue and more recently in relation to wars of intervention. Of themselves they do not say whether a particular war is morally justified or not, but they do give us a set of criteria which must be taken into account in making such a judgement. Nevertheless, this does not preclude, on certain occasions, something more specific.

During the 1960s and 1970s many Christians were critical of the positions being taken by the World Council of Churches in their programme to combat racism. The distinguished American ethicist Paul Ramsey voiced some of their views in his book *Who Speaks for the Church?*[17] In that book he held out as a model of the kind of statement the Church should make what Archbishop Michael Ramsey said in relation to the Unilateral Declaration of Independence by Ian Smith, the Prime Minister of what was then Southern Rhodesia. The Archbishop wrote to Harold Wilson, the British Prime Minister, to say:

> If notwithstanding all efforts there shall come a breakdown and if you and your government should judge it necessary to use force to sustain our country's obligations I am sure a great body of Christian opinion would support you.[18]

For avoidance of doubt, Ramsey later clarified in correspondence exactly what he had said. It was:

> If Rhodesia goes over the brink I agree that it is not for us as Christian Churches to give the government military advice as to what is practicable or possible. That is not our function. But if the British Government thought it

practicable to use force for the protection of the rights of the majority of the Rhodesian people, then I think that as Christians it will be right to use force to that end.[19]

The telegram to the Prime Minister and these words created a major row. There were a number of letters, such as the one from Joost de Blank, the former Archbishop of Capetown, which simply said, 'Of course what you said was absolutely right' and others which lauded his courage. But the majority were vitriolic in their rage. The right wing, and in particular the Christian right wing, unleashed its sanctimonious, abusive hostility.

Ramsey was interviewed on the *Ten O'clock Programme* of the Home Service on 27 October 1965 and again he tried to make his point clear:

I've emphasised the fact – and so did the British Council of Churches emphasise the fact that it is for the Prime Minister and the government to make judgements as to what is really going to be practicable. And what we said was that if in the judgement of the statesmen, it's really practicable to use force in this context, then we believe the Christian conscience should allow the use of force, if it's of the nature of police force in order to forestall and prevent more indiscriminate kinds of force and violence.[20]

What Ramsey said was not platitudinous. Nor, on the other hand, was he advocating a particular policy. He made it quite clear that the decision was the responsibility of the Government. Nevertheless, he offered clear guidance about the moral dimension of this course of action, if the Government decided on it.

That is not the only model of how to speak for God in a secular society, but it is one which does try to recognise the respective responsibilities of government and Church.

This chapter has sought to establish the basis on which the Christian Church approaches the political order and the nature of its voice in the debate. The next will look at the specific issue of law and morality.

Chapter 2

LAW AND MORALITY

THE LAW AND PRIVATE LIFE

The two words 'law' and 'morality' tend, sadly, to have immediately misleading associations in our society. Too often morality brings to mind only sexual morality, and the concept of law is limited to the set of rules needed to help society function. I hope to show that from a Christian point of view both words have a much wider and deeper resonance, and, although not identical, belong together in a fundamental way.

The modern debate about the relationship between law and morality began with the publication of the Wolfenden Report in 1957. At that time all homosexual acts were criminal. The report recommended that consenting acts between adults in private should no longer be a criminal offence. This was accepted, and the subsequent change in the law helped to bring about one of the most significant and lasting changes in our society about morality and its relation to legislation. The recommendation has two key clauses. First, the acts must be 'consenting acts between adults'. In other words, acts involving minors or those who are vulnerable in some way and therefore not able to give informed consent, remain an offence. This emphasis on informed consent has again been a key consideration on a whole range of issues and is one of the most fundamental of our current values. Secondly, the acts must be 'in private'. Consenting sexual acts in public would be offensive to most people, and they therefore remain an offence.

A fundamental assumption of this recommendation is that it is not the duty of the state to impose a particular moral code on society. Morals must be left to individual choice. The state is concerned with what is public and outward, and which therefore impinges on other people. It does not police people's private lives if those lives do not interfere with the legitimate freedom of others.

It is important to note that this assumption, which has been so decisive for the society in which we now live, is fundamentally different from that which still prevails in many parts of the world and which prevailed in the West until the 1960s. The Muslim world, for example, is governed on the basis that there is one revealed law, Sharia, which governs everything in society. There is little separation of the private and the public. Although in the Christian West, the understanding of law was not so unified, for there was a canonical law for the Church, and positive law for the state, that positive law was not a value-free sphere. On the contrary, it expressed basic Christian moral norms which were applicable in what we would regard as private life, as well as public.

The Wolfenden recommendations did not come out of the blue but represent a strand in philosophical thinking that had been gathering momentum ever since the time of John Stuart Mill in the nineteenth century. Mill said, 'The only purpose for which power can rightly be exercised over any member of a civilized community against his will is to prevent harm to others.' But this immediately poses a question. What constitutes harm? Physical hurt is not the only form of harm. Race relations legislation recognises that people can be harmed in other ways. Many would say that an environment in which children can have easy access to pornography is certainly harmful – and this is reflected now in the banning of certain kinds of film on TV, and of other kinds before the 9 p.m. watershed.

Similarly, when the Wolfenden report says that the function of the law is 'to preserve public order and decency, to protect the citizens from what is offensive or injurious and to provide sufficient safeguards against exploitation and corruption of others', almost all the words here – 'decency', 'offensive' and 'corruption' – beg the question of what is meant by them. And when we explore what is meant by them, moral values will be part of the discussion.

THE MORAL BASIS OF LAW

Before that, however, let us explore what might be the basis of law in the first place. Laws are enacted by governments, and before that by rulers. But this in itself cannot be the basis of moral authority for the law, because often in history, and still now, rulers and governments enact laws that are manifestly unjust. In the light of justice, they have later been repealed. It makes no difference whether the laws have been enacted by democratic process or not; the principle still holds, because even democratically elected governments can bring about laws that are later seen to be discriminatory against certain sections of the population. It was not long ago that the laws of this country forbad certain categories of people from voting – Catholics, women, men without property and so on. Indeed, law in a democratic society is in a continuous process of revision. So, in short, there is something beyond law itself, in the light of which we measure and revise laws. Rooted in our sense of what is fair or just, we grope to express what this something beyond might be. For traditional religious believers, it was and is the moral law or moral order.

A good example of the function and necessity of this can be seen in relation to international human rights law. This is a huge achievement, largely dating from the aftermath of World War II. There is now a universal legal benchmark on human rights. But even here, there is something more involved than law. For some countries have not adopted the international covenants – even so, if they act in breach of them we still regard them as violating some fundamental standard. Furthermore, as with domestic law, inter-national law is always open to revision and improvement in the light of a more refined sense of what is fundamentally right. Earlier thinkers made a distinction between *ius gentium* and *ius naturale* – roughly speaking, a distinction between agreements actually in place between nations and the natural law in the light of which all just agreements would be rooted.

I want now to set out the great medieval vision of law, which was fully articulated by Thomas Aquinas and the essentials of which are still held by the Catholic Church. It provides a series of contrasts with the very limited, thin understanding of law held by most moderns. From a Catholic perspective, law originates in the eternal law of God. It is an expression of the Divine wisdom designed to bring about human virtue and endless beatitude. This law is reflected first of all in the natural law, the morality which is basic to human life in community and which is graspable by the human reason. This natural law takes effect in the civil law of the state and also the law of the Church, canon law, with which I am not concerned now. Civil law is derived from natural law in two ways. One, it is 'drawn deductively like conclusions from premises', as Aquinas put it. For example, from natural law we have the general principle that we are not to harm others. This is drawn to its logical conclusion in the law that forbids murder. Secondly, civil legislation is related to natural law as general directions receiving detailed application. For example, natural law lays down that crimes are to be punished, but the exact penalty is left to human judgement. So let us look at some of the contrasts with our meagre modern concept of law.

First, law originates in the Eternal mind. It is not simply a human construct.

Secondly, it has an objective reality. It is not simply a question of each individual human being deciding that some things are right and others wrong, with one opinion being as good as another.

Thirdly, it is rational, designed to indicate what will bring about good consequences and avoid harmful ones. It is not just about command and obedience, feelings of obligation and duty, though these are of course involved. It is, as it were, a rational design for right living and happiness, if we could but see it. It is the rational way to achieve a proper end, the common good of humanity. In the old Book of Common Prayer, just before Christmas, there appear in italics the words, '*O Sapientia*'. It indicates the beginning of the Advent antiphons which were said in the days leading up to Christmas. *O Sapientia* reads:

> O wisdom, coming forth from the mouth of the Most High,
> reaching from one end to the other mightily,
> and sweetly ordering all things:
> Come and teach us the way of prudence.

It sums up, I think, something of this vision of law – it is first of all wisdom, it orders all things sweetly, and it takes root in our lives in the form of prudence, the cardinal virtue or hinge on which all other virtues depend, in that it enables us to balance the many claims upon us.

Fourthly, as the phrase 'natural law' indicates and as that antiphon brings out, it goes wider than what we think of as morality to embrace the laws of nature and aesthetics. There is a wonderful poem by Boethius, the sixth-century philosopher, who expresses this beautifully:

> In regular harmony
> The world moves through its changes;
> Seas in competition with each other
> Are held in balance by eternal laws ...
> Nor may land move out
> And extend its limits.
> What binds all things to order,
> Is love.
> If love's reins slackened
> All things held now by mutual love
> At once would fall to warring with each other
> Striving to wreck that engine of the world
> Which now they drive
> In mutual trust with motion beautiful.
> And love joins peoples too
> By a sacred bond,
> And ties the knot of holy matrimony
> That binds chaste lovers,
> Joins too with its law
> All faithful comrades.
> O happy race of men,
> If the love that rules the stars
> May also rule your hearts![1]

Contrast that with a very familiar modern view that says, of course we need laws to live any kind of life, but these are entirely a matter of human contrivance. Morality is up to each individual, and provided you keep within the law you can do what you want. For Boethius, the Divine ordering embraces nature, beauty and morality. The love that rules the stars is also there to rule our hearts – a line quoted later by Dante.

I am not suggesting that Thomas Aquinas' view of law can stand today without qualification. One fallacy, which has led the Roman Catholic Church into a great deal of trouble over artificial contraception, is the notion that natural law is discovered simply by reading off what happens in nature – in nature natural intercourse leads to the possibility of children, and this is therefore the obligatory course for us. But what is natural for us human beings is to use our God-given human minds, not through imitating nature, but working in relation to nature, for our own and the common good.

The concept of a natural order, or intrinsic moral order in the universe, that can be grasped by rational minds, has been criticised from a number of different points of view. Some of the sixteenth-century reformers and their descendants have rejected the whole idea, on the grounds that it fails to do justice to the fact that the human race is fallen; its mind is darkened and it is therefore incapable of properly grasping what is right or wrong. However, we only have to look at St Paul to see how mistaken that view is. Paul writes:

> When gentiles who do not possess the law [that is, the Jewish Torah, or revealed law of God] carry out its precepts by the light of nature, then, although they have no law, they are their own law; they show that what the law requires is inscribed on their hearts, and to this their conscience gives supporting witness, since their own thoughts argue the case, sometimes against them, sometimes even for them.

> Romans 2:14–15

The concept of natural law, or a moral order that is objective and universal, has also been much criticised from a philosophical point of view. In the light of this, it is clear that some of the assumptions and applications of the old concept of natural law cannot stand, but its essentials – that is, the belief that there is a moral order, rooted in the wisdom of God, which we can apprehend by the use of our minds – I would still want to defend.[2]

The concept of law itself has also been critiqued from a Marxist point of view. Marx said:

> Legislation, whether political or civil, never does more than proclaim, express in words, the will of economic relations.[3]

Now there is clearly a great deal of truth in that. Law in history has been class based, reflecting first the interests of the aristocracy, and then later the interests of the rising bourgeoisie. You only have to look at the history of Trade Union legislation and the decisions of the courts at the beginning of the twentieth century to see the extent of the class bias. So law as we have it, as Marx said, will always to some extent reflect the economic and power realities in the society of that time. For Marx this would only be done away with in a truly communist society. For a Christian, it means that all human laws are always subject to revision and improvement by a higher justice. There is no utopia on this earth. Even the best society will provide only an approximation to some ultimate goal beyond our conceiving. But this underlines the importance of the concept of a moral order, higher than even the best laws, in the light of which all must be open to scrutiny.

Nevertheless, that having been said, I would not want to over-simplify the issue of a natural moral order. Take, for example, the issue of abortion. Now there are some who say, 'I think abortion is wrong, but I respect the fact that this is a democratic society which has decided to allow it in some circumstances. I would never have one myself, but I agree that those who want one and who meet the legal criteria should be allowed to do so.' That is a position which seems relatively unproblematic. However, according to the Roman Catholic Church, abortion is contrary to natural law. In short, it is murder. In no way is it possible to respect or accept a decision which allows for it, even if the decision is a democratic one. It is because of this that Roman Catholic politicians in America have such difficulty with their church. Those who are personally opposed, but seem to accept the fact that the law in America allows abortion, have been excommunicated or threatened with excommunication by their church. The same situation would arise if euthanasia were legalised either there or in this country.

The first point to draw out of this discussion so far, despite the difficulties just described, is that there is an integral connection between law and morality. They are not coterminous, as I will show, but they are integrally related. In essence the fundamental rules which hold our society together, and which we have an obligation to obey, are rooted in moral values and express a moral vision of what it is to be a human being in society. Nothing human is value free – no institution, no work of art, no law. Whether we are aware of it or not, it will reflect the values of the person or community of which it is a part. There is no such thing as a value-free society. The question is: what are its assumptions and presuppositions, and what are the values that lie hidden in them?

A few years ago there was a very famous debate on this subject between the Oxford philosopher, Herbert Hart and a learned law lord, Lord Devlin. Professor Hart argued along the lines of Wolfenden that it is no business of the law to enforce morality. Lord Devlin argued that law actually has morality built into it. In fact, however, both positions need to be qualified. For Hart also believed that a 'shared morality' is essential to any society, and he called for a recognition of 'the minimum content of natural law' – that is, the recognition of certain universal values upon which the law of every society is based. Yet the application of even allegedly universal values is controversial in some respects. The principle of the sanctity of life makes murder a crime. But its application to abortion or euthanasia depends very much on the views of life of the people concerned, views which will usually be rooted in religion as much as morality. There are some very testing issues here for those who are not in sympathy with modern laws which permit actions they regard as immoral.

Devlin argued that the Christian view of marriage – that is, monogamy – has been built into our law. 'It got there because it is Christian, but it remains there because it is built into the house in which we live and could not be removed without bringing it down.' Further, whether or not people are Christians, they are bound to it because it has been adopted by the society in which they live. What this vivid analogy does not spell out is the obvious point that houses can be adapted and extended. The dramatic example of this in recent years has, of course, been the legislation on civil partnerships. In order to deflect criticism, the Government kept saying that civil partnerships are not marriages – but in fact, they reflect, clause by clause, the legislation on marriage. The house of marriage has had an extension. But suppose the character of our society so changed that there was a general push to legalise polygamy, or to avoid charges of sexism, polyandry? That would be a very dramatic change, and would, I suppose, be equivalent to virtually demolishing the house with a view to building a new one in its place – but, however unlikely in practice, it is theoretically conceivable. As argued in the previous chapter, the state is not in fact neutral on the issue of marriage; at the moment it accepts and enshrines in law a Christian understanding of it.

What this means is that the fundamental laws which bind a society together will be rooted in moral principles. Their application in practice may give rise to strong disagreements, and laws can and do change to reflect the moral vision of the society in which they are made. Nevertheless, it is still a moral vision they reflect. The law allowing for civil partnerships was passionately argued for on moral grounds, not just as a matter of expediency.

WHAT IT IS TO BE A HUMAN BEING

A few years ago I was a member of the Home Office Policy Committee for the Reform of the Law on Sexual Offences. We had a range of issues to deal with including prostitution, soliciting, living on immoral earnings, brothels and bestiality. This was in the 1980s and all the members were basically working on the Wolfenden assumption that the law should not try to enforce morality, and that the law was by implication morally neutral. But here we need to be careful, for these two assumptions are not quite synonymous. Although myself sharing the first assumption that the law should not in most cases try to act as a moral policeman, I found myself questioning the second assumption that the law either is or should be totally morally neutral. Take the case of prostitution. Acts of prostitution – that is, offering sex for money – are not in themselves a criminal offence, but a number of other activities associated with prostitution, such as pimping, soliciting and keeping brothels, are. Take soliciting. If it is not illegal to be a prostitute, why should it be illegal to solicit for business? We allow soliciting for all other kinds of things. The law makes it illegal because of the 'nuisance' effect and because it is 'offensive', but as Professor Basil Mitchell has written:

> The mere fact that people are being accosted is not enough to give offence. One is not 'offended' by a pavement artist seeking alms or by a child demanding a penny for the guy. The offence is associated with the knowledge that the soliciting is being done with a view to prostitution and it would not be objected to, or would be objected to very much less, if prostitution were regarded as morally acceptable. An innocent who had no idea what these women were doing would not be offended.

So, as he put it:

> This is one of a number of cases where it is reasonable to suppose that the law is guided by a variety of considerations. The prevention of offence is certainly the principal one, but it is not wholly independent of the moral assessment of the offending acts.[4]

The issue came home to me even more sharply when we were considering bestiality – that is, sexual relationships with animals. Buggery with animals was an offence under the 1956 Sexual Offences Act carrying a maximum sentence of life imprisonment. We were all agreed that the penalties at that time were draconian and needed to be much lighter. But the majority of the committee wanted the offence abolished altogether. They argued that if there was hurt to the animals involved, then people would be caught under the act which forbids cruelty to animals. But it struck me then, and continues to do so, that there is something fundamentally contrary to the dignity of what it is to be a human being in having sexual relationships with animals, and it is perfectly proper for the law to reflect this reaction. In short, the law is not simply about the consequences of acts and whether they harm others, but it enshrines a society's view of what it is to be a human being, and it therefore does criminalise acts that are an affront to that proper dignity.

One of the reasons why our society has, I think, got things wrong on these issues is because since the seventeenth century there has been such an over-individualistic understanding of what it is to be a human being. This atomistic view forgets that we only become and remain persons in relation to other persons. As stated in the previous chapter, mind is a social reality. We are essentially, and not just optionally, always persons in community. Therefore when we are thinking about morality, it is quite one-sided simply to think of this as a matter of individual choice. We are all the product of and shaped by human communities and our very existence as human persons is bound up with such communities. It is right to be concerned with the moral values of those communities as expressed in their public institutions and laws, just as it is right to be concerned with the moral judgements of the individuals who are members of those communities.

Yet, I would still line up on the liberal side on most issues, and this is because in our society we rightly place very great value on the importance of individual choice. People should be given the maximum freedom to make their own choices. So there are two views here. One says that the law is morally neutral, and that morality is a matter of private judgement. I say that the law is not morally neutral. It reflects a particular set of moral values, one imparted to it by the religion and history of the society whose law it is. This is not static, but continually evolving. Nevertheless, it will still be rooted in certain moral assumptions and presuppositions. At the same time, the society in which we live rightly accords the maximum worth to a particular value, that of individual freedom of choice. On a range of issues it will be a matter of balancing the moral assumptions of the society with this freedom. In relation to prostitution, the balance comes down in favour of not criminalising acts of prostitution in themselves but doing so in relation to a range of activities that are associated with prostitution, such as soliciting, pimping and keeping a brothel.

That having been said, morality clearly goes deeper and beyond the law in a number of respects. First, not everything we regard as wrong is a criminal offence. Aquinas asks, 'Is it the business of the law to restrain all vice?' And he gives the answer, 'No.' This is because the law has to take into account the actual capacities of most human beings, and most of us are of a pretty middling moral disposition. If the law tried to control every aspect of human life, we would find it intolerable. The law should confine itself to what is necessary for the stability and cohesion of society. So it forbids only those grave vices which decent people will want to avoid anyway, 'Which the average man can avoid, and chiefly those which do harm to others and have to be stopped if human society is to be maintained, such as murder, theft and so forth.'

So the law does not criminalise every vice, nor according to Aquinas does it prescribe acts of all the virtues. It is concerned only with those virtues that make for the common good. The moral law covers all the virtues, but civil law is limited to what enables society to function. A good example is that of lying. Lying is immoral but the law is concerned only with those lies which impinge on our life together, such as perjury. A man who lies to his wife is immoral. If he lies in court he is both immoral and a criminal.

A different but related reason why the scope of the law is limited, is that law has to be enforced to be any use. If it cannot be enforced, then it is not only useless, but it brings the law itself into disrepute. We might give an example of the prohibition laws against alcohol in the United States in the twentieth century, which were eventually repealed. A contemporary example is legislation in relation to prostitution. There are various laws which try to mitigate the worst evils associated with prostitution, but the act of prostitution itself – that is, selling sex for money – is not a crime, probably on the grounds that such a law could not be enforced.

T. S. Eliot wrote a once-famous book called *The Idea of a Christian Society*. He did not assume that everyone in such a society would be believing Christians. But he did think that Christians within it would be influential in it, shaping its ethos. He said:

> The Christian can be satisfied with nothing less than a
> Christian organization of society – which is not the same
> thing as a society consisting exclusively of devout Christians.
> It would be a society in which the natural end of man –
> virtue and well-being in community – is acknowledged for
> all, and the supernatural end – beatitude – for those who
> have the eyes to see it.[5]

Although that kind of view is not in fashion, it is still worth thinking about. Is what he calls 'the natural end of man – virtue and well-being in community' a goal around which even our multi-faith society could unite? I believe it is worth testing out. Since this is a society in which there is religious freedom, then the supernatural end of man, 'beatitude', would of course be an option 'for those who have eyes to see it'. This issue is pursued further in the final chapter, where it is suggested that today we need a less static and more developmental view of human life, both personal and in society.

That natural end, virtue and well-being in community, does, I think, depend on a much deeper and richer concept of both law and morality than we have in our society at the moment, and I think that we need to draw again on the deep wells of traditional Christian thinking on this subject. It is true that there is a strong move today in some quarters to get away from simply measuring the GNP of a country to consider questions of happiness and well-being. However, the natural end of human life is not simply well-being but virtue, and not just individual well-being but well-being in community.

I suggested at the beginning of this chapter that what bedevils this whole subject is a narrow, stereotypical understanding of morality and a very narrow, pragmatic view of law. I had a sad experience of the former when some years ago I helped mount a conference at Cumberland Lodge on morality and soap operas. I was fortunate in being able to attract some distinguished writers and producers, but failed to get across the message that morality was not primarily about who was having or not having sex. What I wanted people to reflect on were the fundamental assumptions and presuppositions behind the story-lines. For, whether we are aware of it or not, these will carry a moral vision. In fact the moral vision expressed in some soap operas has some strong elements, such as tolerance. It is not a question of thinking about morality in order to judge, but in order to be clear about what we are doing. This needs to be stressed in order to take on board the fact that morality, or a moral vision, is fundamental both to life and to law in all its aspects.

In the international sphere, for example, the idea of human rights is first of all a moral concept.[6] It can and does and should wherever possible take legal form, but still the moral imperative is prior. It is this which enables human rights legislation to be scrutinised and improved. It is this which enables us to judge certain actions as violations of human rights, even though there may be no law in place.

THE CREATION OF A MORAL *MILIEU* AND THE RETURN OF A CONCEPT OF HONOUR

The importance of this moral dimension was brought dramatically to the fore in the recent exposure of expenses being claimed by Members of Parliament. There are a number of elements to this.

First, we have to go back to the origin of the problem. This was the failure of governments, of different political complexions, to raise the pay of Members of Parliament to something roughly equivalent to what many of them might expect to earn outside.

This failure was of course because they feared that we, the public, would not stand it. By many standards, of course, MPs are very well paid, but the fact is that in a competitive market, many could earn more outside. So there was a failure by government and the public to face up to realities.

Secondly, as a result of this, it appears to have been implied that generous allowances would be made for second homes and the expenses associated with them. So a failure to face reality resulted in a subterfuge that lent itself to dishonesty.

Thirdly, the office charged with administering expenses, under the Speaker, seems to have told people they could claim for more or less whatever they wanted. This, again, was a disgraceful abuse of the system, and is in stark contrast to the kind of scrutiny that the Inland Revenue would expect to bring to bear.

Fourthly, within this overall climate, it appears that some claims were downright illegal.

Fifthly, within the total spectrum of revelations, there is a clear distinction to be made between those who acted in a criminal manner; those who stayed within the letter of the law but who, by any ordinary reckoning, were grossly dishonest; those who pushed the limits of what was thought to be legal beyond what most ordinary people would regard as justified; and those whose expense claims were modest and entirely justified. What happened, of course, was that they all, as it were, put up their hands and said, 'Yes, we know the system is wrong, and we must change it.' But this corporate putting up of hands has blurred the fact that there were those huge differences in behaviour that I have just outlined. Whilst it is true that some MPs have resigned or said that they are not going to stand at the next election or have agreed to pay back some money (is that good enough?), there has been some blurring of individual responsibility, with the general smearing of Parliament as a whole. The prophet Ezekiel warned humanity more that 2500 years ago that we are individually responsible, and we cannot hide ourselves behind an appeal to corporate responsibility. Furthermore, this general smearing of MPs is highly detrimental to our national life. A respected and effective Parliament is crucial to our society, and the fact that Members of Parliament are held in low esteem by the general public is unhealthy.

Sixthly, this scandal reveals a moral climate in which people are guided only by what they think is legal, with what is legal being pushed as far as possible, without any thought as to whether it is also honest. For whilst the legal is underpinned by the ethical, what is ethical goes far wider and deeper. The defence of MPs time and again was that they had done nothing illegal. Perhaps they hadn't: but what they had done certainly seemed morally unjustified to most of the rest of the population. Yet, in this respect the moral climate of Parliament is not much different from that of the rest of society. For in recent decades so much of society has been characterised by such an attitude, where the only question being asked is whether something is within the law. The idea that if you stay inside the law what you do is all right, is very widespread. But as the parliamentary scandal has so dramatically shown, this assumption is fundamentally misconceived.

There are now some signs of a reaction against the idea that keeping within the law is enough. As far as the market economy is concerned, for example, its most thoughtful advocates have always argued that it depends on a moral foundation for its success. This has recently been reiterated, for example, by the Reith Lecturer, Professor Sandel, by the banker Stephen Green (who is also a Church of England priest) in his book *Markets and Morals*, and by the Pope in his latest encyclical, *Caritas in Veritate*, who all argue that the market must be seen in a wider moral, and indeed theological, framework. In the field of financial regulation, the best companies have always taken the view that the law is not enough, and have said that the ethos, or moral *milieu* in which people work is even more important. It is not just a question of what is permissible but what is honourable. Indeed, where has the whole concept of honour gone in our society? And honour does not exist in isolation; it is part of and arises out of a community characterised by values which everyone is expected to uphold.

What this analysis reveals is that a moral dimension goes through every aspect of life and law. In particular, it shows that what is legal is not enough. There is a moral law as well as human legislation. The best companies in our society seek to create an ethos or moral *milieu* in which the right thing is done for its own sake, not one in which people push their luck as far as they can stretch the law. What this also brings out is that institutions are now amongst the major carriers of values in our society. The professional associations, the best companies, the best schools seek to create a moral climate in which their members operate. They have a major challenge, because they are operating in a moral climate that believes keeping within the law is all that matters. Good laws express a moral vision, but they do not contain it. The moral vision goes wider and deeper and, for a Christian, is ultimately grounded in the wisdom of God.

WHAT MAKES US THINK GOD WANTS DEMOCRACY?

REINHOLD NIEBUHR'S DEFENCE OF DEMOCRACY

A few years ago the *Observer* newspaper ran a special feature on democracy in which one of the sections was entitled 'Is God Democratic?'[1] The usual suspects gave their answers: yes and no, but mostly with a fairly sceptical tone. That scepticism would be fairly widely reflected in society. First because a quick read of the Bible suggests that by modern standards, God is rather autocratic and authoritarian. Secondly, because we know how easy it is for our religious views simply to reflect the values of the age in which we live. When people believed in autocratic government, especially the divine right of kings, it was natural to think of God in these terms. Now most of us in the West advocate some form of democracy, and it is proper to be suspicious of any claim to see God in more democratic terms and backing democracy.[2] Nevertheless, despite that suspicion, I make that claim here. I will be pursuing it, especially through the most famous defence of democracy from a Christian in modern times, that by Reinhold Niebuhr, and then I will look at some more recent approaches.[3]

The nature of democracy, its strengths, weaknesses and Christian justification, was a lifelong interest for Niebuhr. It was, however, in *The Children of Light and the Children of Darkness*, published in 1945, that his thought on this subject received its most systematic formulation. It also contained his famous aphorism:

> Man's capacity for justice makes democracy possible; but man's inclination to injustice makes democracy necessary.[4]

In 1944 he was gloomy about the prospects of democracy in a post-war world and wrote *The Children of Light and the Children of*

Darkness to provide a stronger basis for it than it had hitherto had, and one which in the American context would help the revival of Americans for Democratic Action (the ADA), the leftish political movement in which he was a key member. 'It was a reassuring vision for a time of liberal rebuilding.'[5]

Niebuhr was sufficiently influenced by Marxist analysis to recognise that from one point of view, the rise of liberal democracy was an expression of bourgeois interests breaking the stranglehold of a feudal order dominated by the aristocracy and the Church. As he put it:

> The most pathetic aspect of the bourgeois faith is that it regards its characteristic perspectives and convictions as universally valid and applicable, at the precise moment in history when they are being unmasked as the peculiar convictions of a special class which flourished in a special situation in western society.[6]

Yet he also believed that democracy expressed values of abiding validity. The freedom of subjects to choose their own governments and the equality associated with this, so that in the political order one counts for one, neither more nor less, was, he argued, fundamental to both a Christian and a secular view of existence. Moreover, this freedom, expressed in economic terms through the market, and in other ways, allowed creative possibilities for the future to emerge. Much that was wrong might come about as well, but taking this risk was better than blocking developments that might enhance human life and well-being.

The justification of democracy in the first part of Niebuhr's aphorism, 'Man's capacity for justice makes democracy possible', was, in Niebuhr's view, inadequate by itself, for it was based on an over-optimistic Enlightenment view of humanity which assumed that conflicts could always be resolved and progress achieved. Hence the sub-title of *The Children of Light and the Children of Darkness* is 'A Vindication of Democracy and a Critique of its Traditional Defenders'. For Niebuhr the best vindication of democracy was based on an awareness of our tendency to oppress one another and the consequent need to control political power. Hobbes and Luther both had a realistic sense of the way human beings do violence to one another, and from this followed their call for strong government to stop people tearing themselves apart. What they failed to point out is that potentially the biggest oppressor of all is government itself; hence the paramount need to have some way of checking, balancing and controlling it. From this springs the classical separation of powers into the executive, the legislature and the judiciary, together with fixed elections and other mechanisms.

In Niebuhr's classic defence of liberal democracy, the 'children of light' are Western thinkers of the Enlightenment and their followers in subsequent ages, who believed there was a capacity for altruism in human beings, who argued that real progress could be made in the human lot and who thought that through education and reason most problems could be solved and most disputes settled. For Niebuhr, this was all foolishness. The 'children of darkness' are wiser, because they know the power of human egoism and the ineluctable tendency of human beings to expand their interests at the expense of others; but they are children of darkness because in their moral cynicism they act as though this is the only force at work. The only sound basis for democracy is one that takes our tendency to human aggrandisement at the expense of others realistically into account, but which sets this in a moral framework provided by the children of light. So, as he put it:

> The preservation of a democratic civilization requires the wisdom of the serpent and the harmlessness of the dove. The children of light must be armed with the wisdom of the children of darkness but remain free of their malice. They must know the power of self-interest in human society without giving it moral justification. They must have this wisdom in order that they may beguile, deflect, harness and restrain self-interest, individual and collective, for the sake of the community.[7]

Niebuhr argued that historically democracy was the joint achievement of Christian and secular thought, forms of Calvinism and Christian sects on the one hand and rationalists on the other. He also believed that Christianity contributes three insights of permanent validity. First, a basis for authority outside government itself, as expressed in the biblical notion that we are called to obey God rather than Caesar. Secondly, a non-instrumental view of human beings. All individuals are of value in themselves for themselves, and must never be treated simply as a cipher in a larger scheme of things. And thirdly, an awareness of our human sin, whereby the ordinary struggle to survive is turned into a drive for prestige and power. This is the insight that liberal idealists totally failed to see.

He also believed that Marxists were guilty of the same naivety about human nature, for though they believed in the class struggle until a truly communist society came into being, they thought that in such a society all conflict would be resolved, because its basis in an unjust economic order would have been corrected. But they ignored the fact that economic power, however important, is not the only form of power, and the human will to power remains even in a society where economic inequalities have been done away with.

So Western liberals, both secular and Christian, and Marxists, share an over-optimistic view of human nature. As Niebuhr put it:

> The facts about human nature which make a monopoly of
> power dangerous and a balance of power desirable are
> understood in neither theory but are understood from the
> standpoint of Christian faith.[8]

Niebuhr's justification of democracy from that point of view is as pertinent today as it was then. But his classic aphorism has two parts to it, not only the statement that 'man's inclination to injustice makes democracy necessary', but also that 'man's capacity for justice makes democracy possible'. The question I wish to consider is whether there is not a stronger Christian basis for 'man's capacity for justice makes democracy possible' than Niebuhr himself put forward.

This capacity for justice has three aspects to it: liberty, equality and the social nature of human life, as will be argued in the next chapter.

Few would disagree that the first and most fundamental value of liberal democracy is individual freedom. This basic liberty includes a range of freedoms: freedom of speech, of worship and of assembly, for example. But it certainly includes freedom to choose those by whom we will be governed.

We now take this so much for granted that we forget how new this is, and how until comparatively recently the Roman Catholic hierarchy in some countries opposed democracy. It is important to see why they might have done this. For if God is a Divine Ruler who has revealed his law to us, it is natural to think that this pattern should be reflected in human rulers, and obedience to their law. Hierarchy and obedience are, as it were, written into the very constitution of the universe. And this, in itself, can provide a very beautiful vision for the ordering of both the cosmos and society. So it is easy to see how democracy, in the sense of rule of the people, by the people, for the people, might be regarded as inimical to it.

C. S. Lewis, like Niebuhr, argued that we need democracy in our fallen, sinful state, because we can never trust human rulers. But, he argued, this is a concession. In a perfect, unfallen world we would have hierarchy and obedience. He argued that our real hunger is for inequality. 'The man who has never wanted to kneel or bow is a prosaic barbarian', he wrote.[9] This desire for inequality, he argued, is reflected in the adulation we give to heroes and superstars, and why right-wing dictatorships can gain adherents. We do indeed need democracy in this world; nevertheless, 'there is no spiritual substance in flat equality'. We should recognise that 'under the necessary outer covering of legal equality, the whole hierarchical dance and harmony of our deep and joyously accepted spiritual inequalities should be alive.'

However, we can hugely admire someone, in their spiritual qualities, without this leading to either prostration or obedience. Rather, admiration leads to a desire to learn from and be influenced by the person. Furthermore, it will almost certainly be a characteristic of the person we admire that they precisely do not want us to kneel and obey them. They will want us to gain our own insights and find our own way. Nicholas Ferrar, who founded the religious community at Little Gidding in the seventeenth century, based on his family, wrote to his niece, 'I purpose and hope by God's grace to be to you not as a master but as a partner and fellow student.' Such an attitude is rooted in a faith that believes God has come amongst us in Jesus as brother and partner in God.

Although Locke, one of the seminal thinkers for the development of democracy, was a Christian believer and his view of both government and human rights is based on the reality of God, subsequent theorists have detached the theological foundations of this and argued for the legitimacy of Locke's views in themselves, irrespective of whether they are undergirded by a creator in whose image we are made. Related to this is the fact that despite the serious Christian faith of Locke and a good number of other Enlightenment thinkers, many people persist in seeing the Enlightenment as a secular achievement. We need to understand why this is so.

Kingship is the prime model for rule in the Scriptures. If the Enlightenment is seen in terms of the rejection of kingship, at least in its absolute form, then it is easy to see how the emergence of democracy might be seen as primarily a secular achievement. So it is necessary to probe the kingship model to see what it does and does not imply.

The dominance of the kingship metaphor, at its best, allows for the C. S. Lewis view that in heaven there is rule by a Divine King who is totally given over to our good, but that we need democracy now because no human ruler can be trusted. This was a view also expressed on BBC Radio 4 in a 'Thought for the Day' on 6 September 2008 by Joel Edwards, who speaks for a good number of evangelicals. He said that in the present, here on earth, 'God does democracy', but 'In Biblical terms God's ideal would be a theocracy in which all aspects of human relationships come immediately under his rule and sovereignty.' However, this is just the kind of contrast that we need to question. For if democracy is just a temporary expedient, a concession to our human weakness, due to be done away with when the rule of the perfect Divine King is established, I wonder whether it provides a firm enough foundation for a truly Christian polity?

A parallel can be made with another human institution – marriage. Jesus is reported to have said that in heaven there is neither marrying nor giving in marriage, but we are like the angels. Now it is true that in heaven there will be no need for procreation, one of the purposes of marriage. But this does not mean the end of deep and intimate relationships. There is no marrying or giving in marriage because in a sense everyone will be married to everyone else; there will be a deep and intimate communion within the body of Christ not only with Christ himself, but in him with all other members of the body. So whilst there is one aspect of marriage for which there is no continuing purpose in heaven, there is another which finds its fulfilment there. Can we say the same about democracy?

In so far as democracy exists to check and stop the emergence of despotic rule, there is indeed no need for it in heaven, for there all is perfected. But there is another aspect of democracy, and that is the natural coming together of human beings to order their common life. This is the emphasis in democracy going back to the ancient Greeks and preserved in the Catholic, if not always in the Reformed, tradition. If this is a fundamental feature of what it means to be a human being, and not just a concession to either finitude or sin, then perhaps, like marriage, it finds its proper fulfilment in heaven, in ways of course which we cannot now imagine.

Lewis and many others suggest that because God is the perfect King, who desires only the well-being of his subjects, there is no need for any form of government other than that. But this is to misunderstand the relationship between divine and human activity, and to suggest that they are mutually exclusive accounts of human behaviour.

God has bestowed on us the awesome gift of freedom. He has taken the risk of putting things in our hands. If this gift of freedom is fundamental to God's intention for us, what indeed helps to define us as human beings, then it would seem odd that this is a gift only for this life, as though we have it now, and then it is taken away from us. A better approach is to say, not that it is taken away from us, but that in heaven, made perfect in a *milieu* of intimate communion with the Divine Presence, that freedom is exercised rightly.

Furthermore, heaven is a society, a communion of saints; but still a society. And, as Austin Farrer used to emphasise, the Divine Presence that fully enfolds us is met in and through that society; in and through the body of Christ, the communion of fellow believers.

It can also be pointed out that the image of kingship is not the only one suggested by the New Testament. Jesus said to his followers that in the Kingdom they will sit on thrones judging the twelve tribes of Israel. There was a period in the history of Israel when it was judges, rather than kings, that arbitrated and ordered the common life. So it may be that God, without ceasing to be King, delegates the ordering of the common life in heaven as he does on earth. His kingship, in other words, does not just consist of each individual before the throne, but human beings in communion with one another, sharing responsibility for their common life before the throne. God rules, in the sense that the whole body of Christ moves in perfect harmony with his purpose. But that body has a properly delegated function, shared responsibility for the common life.

All this is very speculative but what it suggests is that there are elements in liberal democracy which are not just here for the interim, a concession to finitude and sin, but which, however impossible to picture, have their proper grounding and fulfilment in heaven. The reason for making such a suggestion is to counter the suspicion that democracy is really a secular achievement rooted in secular political philosophy. Furthermore, it may be that whilst the emphasis Niebuhr gave to 'man's inclination to injustice' was a necessary corrective and a permanent insight, he did not give a strong enough theological grounding to the Enlightenment stress on 'man's capacity for justice'. This is in part because his own emphasis is rooted in a Protestant understanding of the state as a concession to human sin, rather than the Catholic understanding that it is natural and right for human beings to come together to order their common life.

OLIVER O'DONOVAN'S CAUTION ABOUT DEMOCRACY

I now consider what Oliver O'Donovan has written on democracy. I do so because he offers a learned and deeply challenging critique of the whole tradition of Western thinking about the basis of democracy, including both aspects of Niebuhr's aphorism. His alternative approach is very wide ranging and it is possible here to consider only what he writes under the heading of 'legitimation'. There is for O'Donovan a fundamental distinction between good government, which he is prepared to call liberal government, and liberal democracy. He describes, without arguing for, good government in the following terms:

> This account has a number of elements, all to do with responsiveness to the real and felt needs of society: an elected parliament as a formal court of pleas; local representative organs with local autonomy; the admission of open and candid speech on all matters relating to the common good; the obligation of government to natural and divine law; the recognition of basic individual rights at law as a limiting constraint upon inequalities of social order; the independence of courts from executive interference; due forms of consultation and deliberation in preparing legislation and due process for promulgating it, and so on.[10]

For him the key question is how far this kind of good government is dependent on its legitimation through democratic elections. He suggests that election is neither a necessary nor a sufficient condition. There have been good governments without elections, and elections that have resulted in unjust governments. He then considers three ways in which democratic elections might be considered integral. The first claims that democratic elections are implicit in the very idea of good liberal government, as it were, the second stage of a developing idea. He rejects this on the grounds that in fact what we are left with is 'the humdrum practice of voting in elections',[11] which seems very far from the kind of grand claims made for liberal democracy about regenerating society. There is a very great deal wrong with Western-style democracies at the moment, but when we are feeling disillusioned, one of the pictures we need to bear in mind is that of black South Africans queuing for hours in order to cast their votes in a system that for the first time allowed their votes to count.

One aspect of the democratic idea that O'Donovan does not seem to consider is the gradual widening out of the franchise until it became universal. Previously excluded groups such as Roman Catholics, Jews, men without property, women as a whole, and then women below the age at which men were allowed to vote, over the course of 100 years or so were enabled to share in the process of electing their government. The key moral idea here is that one counts for one, neither more, nor less. O'Donovan rightly bases his idea of equality on the equal dignity and worth of all human beings in the eyes of God, and rightly believes this has important political implications, like equality before the law. Whilst again, rightly, he is anxious to avoid any flat notion of equality which fails to take into account the different gifts and vocations which society needs for its flourishing, he seems strangely blind to the outworking of the Christian idea of equality in the idea of one person one vote. If people are to be consulted about the government they want, then there can be no basis for denying that the perspective on life and views of every individual ought to be taken into account on an equal basis.

Secondly, there is the claim that liberal democracy ensures just government, and here he quotes Niebuhr. But, he argues, this can only be that envisaged by the contractarian myth, which sees political authority as derived from a founding act of popular will. Otherwise we would not look to *democracy* to achieve justice but to intra-governmental 'checks and balances'. The power of an electorate to dismiss and choose its rulers can only be a guarantee of good government, if good government is understood as that which rulers exercise under the authority of the popular will.[12]

Here we note in passing that in his chapter on 'The Powers of Government' he is concerned to stress the unity of governmental power, rather than its threefold expression in the executive, the legislature and the judiciary. Whilst he does not deny the threefold dispensation, his stress on the rightness and inevitability of the unity of government is open to the charge that it weakens the effect of the separation of powers as a check and balance on the unbridled power of the executive.

More substantially, we have to note his deep hostility to what he calls the contractarian myth and to ask if this is really necessary. If the concern is to safeguard the fact that government is ultimately given by and accountable to God, the contractarian myth does not necessarily rule that out. Furthermore, Christians regard themselves as accountable both to God and to one another within the body of Christ. When they come to the Sunday Eucharist, they come accountable for the week just past, not just before God but before one another. This sense of accountability before other human beings can be and ought to be even stronger in office-holders in the Church. So there is no incompatibility in saying that governments are accountable both to God and to the people who elect them. If the people who elect them find them wanting, then they have the right to look for a different government. That new government is also accountable to God, and from a theological point of view is given by God.

The fact is that while popular election by itself is not a guarantee of just government, it is one key element along with others, such as the separation of powers and human rights guaranteed by law, which helps to prevent tyranny. The fact is that there is no way of guaranteeing good government. Democracies can and are manipulated in all kinds of ways, as we see at the moment in Russia and many other countries. The alliance of political power with big money, leading to control or heavy manipulation of the media, with weak processes of law for safeguarding human rights, is a sad reality. But it would be even sadder without the possibility of the electorate bringing in an alternative government *in extremis.*

The third claim which O'Donovan considers, the most modest one, is that elections guarantee that those who are elected are genuinely representative of the electorate. He argues, to the contrary, that election is no such guarantee, as we see in the case of the European institutions. In the European Union, there are elections, but people feel very distant from the bodies to which they have elected people.

For O'Donovan representation is primarily a matter of the imagination. However, being able to envisage someone representing us assumes our willingness – that is, our free choice – to so imagine: in other words, free elections. It can also be pointed out that the European institutions are comparatively recent, and it could be that in the future people will feel more identified with them than they are now. They would be even less likely to do this if there were no elections.

So in the end O'Donovan comes to make a very limited claim indeed for liberal democracy.

> The case for democracy is that it is specifically appropriate to Western societies at this juncture. It is a moment in the Western tradition; it has its own ecological niche. This allows us no universal claims of the 'best regime' kind, nor does it permit the imperial view that the history of democracy is the history of progress. Yet, within its own terms it allows us to be positive about democracy's strengths. The best regime is precisely that regime that plays to the virtues and skills of those who are governed by it; and this one serves us well in demanding and developing certain virtues of bureaucratic and public discourse that the Western tradition has installed. It is our tradition; we are bred in it; we can, if we are sensible about it, make it work.[13]

The rejection of imperialist claims is welcome indeed; nevertheless, I believe this very limited claim is too modest. First, there is the question of the universal franchise, which I have argued is one inescapable implication of believing in the equal worth and dignity of every single individual human being. It is noticeable that a number of countries with traditional political regimes are now inching their way towards this, and some Muslim scholars argue that it is an essential development of two Islamic ideas. The first is the tradition of *ijtihad*, which allows for creative reinterpretations of traditional legal texts in response to modern needs. The second is the institution of the consultative assembly, *Majlis al-Shura*. It is well established that rulers should consult with their leading men and institutions. So it has been argued by Muslim scholars that a true consultative assembly would allow for full democracy.

Secondly, whilst the election of governments is no guarantee that the government so elected will act justly, for populations can be manipulated, it is one element, along with others, that seeks to act as a brake on tyrannous tendencies.

That said, there is one development that is no less crucial and in some respects more so than elections, and that is the guarantee of human rights by law. This is necessary in liberal democracies in order to protect minorities from the tyranny of the majority and to protect individuals from being harmed as a result of 'reasons of state', however rationally justified. In non-democratic societies, where women in particular may be severely disadvantaged, the entrenchment of human rights in law is an even more pressing priority than governments by election, though it is highly likely that the latter will lead to the establishment of the former, not least because women will have the vote.

I suggest that there are elements in liberal democracies that have a wider moral relevance than O'Donovan allows, and this is taken up below.

DEMOCRACY AS A VISION OF WHAT SOCIETY SHOULD BECOME

Until the resurgence of Islam, the major critique of liberal democracy was provided by Marxism. As Marx put it, democracy meant no more than 'the opportunity of deciding once in three or six years which member of the ruling class was to misrepresent the people.' For Marxism the rise of democracy was simply the rise of rule by bourgeois interests, and this would rightly and inevitably be replaced by rule by working-class interests. However, you do not need to be a thoroughgoing Marxist to recognise the element of economic interest at work in political life. Niebuhr was certainly highly aware of that: but what is important to recognise is that with globalisation, economic power is even more powerful now than it was in his time. Behind the press, behind party funding, behind advertising, behind the organisation that wins elections, sadly, even behind some legal judgements in court, lies money: the interests of finance and business. And in the modern world, with so much finance being on a global scale, the power of government to control the movement of money is much weaker.

Figures worldwide suggest that whatever improvements are being made in the lives of the poorest, this imbalance is in fact growing. This highlights two factors. First, the crucial importance of governments acting for the common good. In a world where economic power on a global scale reigns supreme, this will mean that political power needs to be used not just to facilitate business, but to enable the most marginalised to share in the full life of their society.

Secondly, it highlights a distinction made by John de Gruchy between 'democracy as a *vision* of what society should become, and democracy as a *system* of government that seeks to enable the realization of that vision within particular contexts.'[14]

De Gruchy finds the foundation for a Christian vision of democracy in the eighth-century BC prophets, with their conviction about social equality, freedom and justice, and the development of these in five trajectories. First, in the Messianic hope of true liberation for all people from all that oppresses; secondly, in the medieval championing of the common good and the development of trade guilds and other expressions of civil society; thirdly, in the Reformation concept of covenantal obligation, whereby human beings are called to accountable responsibility both to God and to one another; fourthly, the other more radical Reformation emphasis on individual freedom and the separation of Church and state; fifthly, in modern liberation theology, which seeks to overcome economic injustice and oppression.

This distinction between democracy as a vision and democracy as a system is an important one and it reminds us that democracy must always be seen as an ongoing project towards the realisation of that vision. We note, from recent years, the civil rights movement and the different aspects of the struggle for equality for women, which has been part of that quest for full and equal participation by all members of society. The fact that modern Western politics is now so characterised by one-issue campaigns is no bad thing, for it is an indication of other groups – for example, the disabled or children – struggling for their proper place.

AMARTYA SEN'S WIDER VISION

One of the most distinguished public thinkers of our time, the Nobel prize-winner Amartya Sen, has recently put forward a major alternative to the dominant theories of democracy in the West. The dominant theories take a contractarian form – that is, they envisage an ideal scenario in which there is a contract between rulers and people. The most influential modern form of this is that associated with the philosopher John Rawls. Rawls assumes a situation in which none of us know what situation in life we would be born into. We have to choose the ideal society, as it were, blind. On this scenario the only principles on which there could be universal agreement, and therefore a universal sense of fairness, would be first of all, fundamental freedoms for all, and every position open to everyone, irrespective of the status into which they had been born. Furthermore, it would be a society in which any inequalities that arose would be justified only on the basis that they helped the weakest and most vulnerable members of that society.

Sen's starting point is Rawls, and the concept of justice as fairness.[15] But apart from the emphasis on fairness, he is highly critical of Rawls' political philosophy, not least because it assumes a political community for its implementation, whereas today the need is for justice on a global scale, even though there is no global political community. Instead of taking the Enlightenment contractarian approach, he prefers the other Enlightenment approach associated with Adam Smith and others. This posits the need for the impartial spectator to scrutinise our parochial understandings of justice. So fundamental to Sen's approach is the need to listen to, and to take into account all voices, wherever they come from. This is because they represent interests that need to be taken into account, and because they critique and enlarge our own limited perspective.

Also fundamental to Sen is his strong conviction that theories of justice must have a direct bearing on the critical issues facing us today. From that point of view the 'transcendental institutional' approach of Rawls and other contractarians is useless. Our need is to compare and assess relative states of justice and these pictures of an ideal state shed no light on this exercise.

Again, fundamental to Sen's approach is the emphasis on public reasoning. Reasoning, even more than elections, is what democracy is about, and from this point of view democracy can be found elsewhere (for example, in India), even before the Western Enlightenment.

This approach of Sen is a highly valuable corrective to dominant notions and there is much in it with which Christians will resonate. It is noteworthy that Sen points to Jesus' parable of the Good Samaritan to underline his point that in a global world anyone in need is our neighbour, and democracy is fundamentally about listening to our neighbour and taking her or his voice into account.

Nevertheless, whilst accepting his valuable corrective and his proper emphasis on democracy as a form of public reasoning which takes every voice into consideration, and his point that democracy is not simply an achievement of the Western Enlightenment, we can still press the question about whether in practice there is a fairer way of doing this than through elections. On Sen's view democracy is not limited by the ballot box. In a global world, governments should listen to all voices, not just their own electorate, but nevertheless with their own electorate the final and least unfair test must be an election.

Given the distinction between democracy as a vision and democracy as a system, is there anything in the system as it has so far been developed, *contra* Oliver O'Donovan, which is absolutely fundamental, and crucial to stand up for? Even given its present manifest flaws, does the system safeguard some essential insights into what it is for us human beings to live in society? Or are we to say that this is the system that has developed in our society and a good number of others, but other systems may be just as good for rather different kinds of society?

The word 'democracy' has been claimed by a good number of societies we would judge undemocratic. As T. S. Eliot wrote:

> When a term has become so universally sanctified as 'democracy' now is, I begin to wonder whether it means anything, in meaning too many things ... If anybody ever attacked democracy, I might discover what the word meant.[16]

I think meaning can be given to liberal democracy, and it is worth standing up for. One essential element in a liberal democracy, the rule of law and the right to a fair trial, all that we mean by *habeas corpus*, does not belong to democracy alone. It is essential to democracy, and where it fails, as in Iraq so far, democracy fails. But it is not unique to democracy. Islamic societies too insist on the rule of law. Of course questions arise about how far the judiciary is independent from the executive. Such independence is a mark of a democratic system, but even in an Islamic society there is a measure of independence. But what about other features of liberal democracy in relation to Islam?

It has been suggested that what we should look for in the Muslim world are political systems that allow for government by consent. It is certainly important that we should not simply think of the imposition of secular Western liberal ideals on Islamic societies. Nevertheless, given this caution, I think we have to go further and argue that liberal democracies stand not only for government by consent, but they look to obtain that consent in a particular way, by universal franchise, and as mentioned above, there are some Muslim scholars who now argue for this. Another mark is the genuine separation of powers, with a truly independent judiciary safeguarding the rule of law against arbitrary decrees of government, and the separation of the executive from the legislature.

These are not of course the only essential features. There are also fundamental rights and freedoms such as freedom of speech and the press, freedom of assembly and freedom to form political parties. Human rights are not simply an add-on to democracy but fundamental to it. This is because of what Alexis de Tocqueville called the despotism or tyranny of the majority. It is possible in a democracy for the majority view to be elected to government, and then for that government to oppress various minority interests. Those fundamental human interests need to be protected.

When it comes to social and economic rights, as opposed to political rights, their realisation depends significantly on the state of development of that society. But the rights of individual people – of women, of gay and lesbian people and the disabled, and in particular their right to be protected from cruel and demeaning treatment – are fundamental and we cannot take the view that one society's attitude to them is just as good as another's.

There is a danger that if we start making value judgements that some things are better than others, we can slip over not only into arrogance, but into a crusade mentality. Some of President Bush's rhetoric before the Iraq war had something of this about it. What is necessary is the ability to make value judgements – to say, yes, liberal democracy does safeguard certain essentials about what it is for human beings to live in society and to stand up for these in peaceful ways – but always aware that democracy as we know it is very flawed, and even at its best it is only a proximate good, a project towards the realisation of a vision. One of the great strengths of the whole of Niebuhr's writings, not least his prayers, was his ability to make clear judgements whilst at the same time avoiding any suggestion of moral superiority.

Democracy came out of the Enlightenment from the work of Christian as well as secular thinkers, and it expresses a Christian understanding of what it is to be a human being in society, a social being, who is at once made in the image of God and a violator of that image. Christianity has of course lived under a range of different kinds of government, and democracy, as we know, is open to the criticism today, as Eliot put it in the 1930s, that 'what we have is not democracy, but financial oligarchy'.[17] But all qualifications notwithstanding, it does stand for something. It does contain features that safeguard certain fundamental insights into a proper understanding of what it is to be a human being in society.

However, Niebuhr was conscious that democracy is the product of a long and painful history in America and Britain, in which various essential factors for the emergence of democracy were present. These were not yet there in a number of countries.

Democratic self-government is indeed an ultimate ideal of political community. But it is of the greatest importance that we realise that the resources for its effective functioning are not available to many nations.[18]

Again, although he saw democracy as the least bad political system we have so far evolved, he warned strongly against making it into an idol. He thought that America had developed an uncritical, almost religious attitude towards it which was dangerous.

> If one may judge by the various official pronouncements and commencement speeches, Americans have only one religion: devotion to democracy ... democracy is worth preserving. It is a worthy object of qualified loyalty. But is it a proper object of unqualified loyalty? Does not the very extravagance of our devotion prove that we live in a religiously vapid age, in which even Christians fail to penetrate to the more ultimate issues of life?[19]

Democracy is worthy of a qualified loyalty, but we have to realise what it is, 'a method of finding proximate solutions for insoluble problems'.[20] What is fatal is to think that what it offers are final solutions.

Our knowledge that there is no complete solution for the problem would save us from resting in some proximate solution under the illusion that it is an ultimate one.[21]

This means that the balances struck in a democratic society, for example between government control and individual initiatives, or between individual property and state intervention, will always be temporary and have to be re-struck in the light of new problems. So democracy is not a final solution to human problems; nevertheless, as a proximate one, I would argue that it contains features that are vital to the political life of every human society.

LIBERTY, EQUALITY AND HUMAN COMMUNITY

The programme behind the French Revolution of 1789 was based on *Liberté, Egalité, Fraternité.* These three ideas have been the driving force behind political developments in the West ever since the seventeenth century and are still a potent force in the world today. It is often assumed that these are secular ideas, ideas which have sometimes seemed to work against cherished Christian principles. I hope to show that they have a firm Christian grounding, and that the Christian faith has important insights to contribute to their proper understanding.

LIBERTY

The concept of liberty has many aspects, but its first and most fundamental sense is that we human beings are capable of free, rational choice, and that God respects the choices we make. Our freedom to choose may be much more circumscribed than we think because of our genetic makeup and early formation. There is also the age-old philosophical problem of determinism and free-will, which is beyond the scope of this book. Nevertheless, that we are in some profound sense able consciously to shape our future is integral to what it means to be a moral being and, from a Christian point of view, what it means to be made in the image of God. No less important, however, is the seriousness with which God takes our choices, and the respect Jesus showed for them, as revealed, for example, in the story of the temptations in the wilderness. There is a famous scene in Dostoevsky's great novel *The Brothers Karamazov* where Christ returns to earth and confronts the Grand Inquisitor.

The Grand Inquisitor, far from being apologetic for the horrors carried out in the name of Christ, turns on Christ and accuses him of treating human beings as free, when in fact this freedom was too great a burden for them. So, as he says:

> We have corrected your great work and have based it on *miracle, mystery, and authority*. And men rejoiced that they were once more led like sheep and that the terrible gift which had brought them so much suffering had at last been lifted from their hearts.[1]

This fundamental freedom is one which we can exercise, however constricted our outward circumstances might be. It belongs to the dignity of human beings that even when unjustly imprisoned, our spirit is free, and we can think thoughts and develop attitudes that defy our captors and raise us above them.

My theme, however, is not this fundamental freedom, about which much could be said, not least on how it relates to our liberty in Christ as expressed in the well-known line of a prayer: 'In thy service is perfect freedom.' My concern here is freedom as a political idea. However, a question does arise about the relationship, if any, between this fundamental freedom we have as human beings and the various political freedoms we value. After all, it would be possible to say that if we have this fundamental freedom of the spirit even in prison, of what consequence are political freedoms? Is there any connection between them? I believe there is. For if we respect the freedom to choose of other human beings, we will also value enlarging their freedom of choice. Young children only have very limited options open to them. They have to conform to their families' norms. They have to go to school. As they grow up their freedom to choose is widened out, so that parents will let them choose which career to follow and which person to marry. The freedom which God gives to us, and respects, is not less than that which a parent gives to her adult child. As the psalmist puts it: 'Thou hast not shut me up into the hand of the enemy: but hast set my feet in a large room' (Ps. 31:9).

Now issues obviously arise about how large this room ought to be; about how widely the range of choices open to us should be extended or constricted. There are a range of issues on which government now takes action to reduce the choices we have; smoking in public rooms is the obvious one, but there are many others concerning alcohol, drugs and, increasingly, food. But in general we think that it is a mark of a mature person that they can cope with a wide range of choices, and that we ought to respect people's ability to make the right ones. Libertarians, of course, put all their emphasis on leaving people free, whether they are social libertarians, thinking of the choices we make on social issues, or economic libertarians, who champion an unrestricted free market of goods and services.

The first freedom to be fought for in the seventeenth century was freedom of religion; freedom to believe and practise the faith of one's choice. In this country the struggle for religious freedom has been a long and painful one. It is also sobering for those who look to religions themselves to encourage tolerance, for the story is not so much one of enlightened religious people bringing about religious freedom for those with whom they disagreed, but too often religious tolerance coming about because of the pressure of political events and for political reasons. The last time religious passions erupted in violence in this country was in the Civil War of the seventeenth century. There is a sense in which, as a result of that war, they blew themselves out. The Restoration of the monarchy in 1660, followed by the so-called Glorious Revolution of 1688, and then the Act of Toleration of 1689 which allowed Baptists and Presbyterians who were loyal to the Crown to have their own places of worship, expressed an overwhelming sense that anything was better than a religious-based conflict. Tolerance became a political necessity. It was a matter of profound conviction for some Christians like Milton and Locke, whom I will discuss in a moment, but it was political pragmatism that made it a reality. So it was with Catholic Emancipation in 1829. Peel, the Prime Minister, had opposed it and thought it was harmful, but he fought hard to obtain it because he believed that civil war in Ireland would follow without it. Serious civil strife would ensue if Daniel O'Connell, a Catholic, was not allowed to sit in the Parliament to which he had been elected, and this, Peel judged, would be worse than letting Catholics sit. So only gradually, element by element, have the disabilities of non-Anglicans been removed over the last three centuries, and there is of course still the very complex and tangled question of the monarch not being allowed to be or to marry a Catholic.

Article 18 of the Universal Declaration of Human rights says:

> Everyone has the right to freedom of thought, conscience and religion; this right includes freedom to change his religion or belief, and freedom either alone or in community with others and in public or private, to manifest his religion or belief in teaching, practice, worship and observance.

This right is expressed in similar words in a number of other key documents, such as the European Convention.

Sadly, though lip service is often paid to the UN declaration, and its provisions have been signed up to in separate covenants by many countries, there are still too many manifest gross violations of the right to religious freedom.

Although, as I have implied, it is possible to see this gradual progress towards freedom of religion as expressing a desire to prioritise civil peace above issues of religious truth, it is important to remember that at the fountain-head of this stream for both Britain and the United States were John Milton and John Locke. Both put forward arguments on specifically Christian grounds, namely that genuine religious faith must be a matter of personal conviction, and has to be freely chosen, not coerced. A faith that is forced is not true faith. So a context in which people are genuinely free to choose their religion is fundamental to religious faith itself. Locke allows a distinction between a government's legitimate role in dealing with questions of material existence, where a degree of coercion may sometimes be necessary, and questions of belief in which coercion has absolutely no place. This has led to a distinction between the public and the private sphere, and the confinement of religion, for so many, to the personal, private and inner realm. But this distinction is problematical. How can religion, which claims to offer truths of the utmost importance about life, limit itself in that way? As is well known, Islam cannot see itself as so limited or confined in scope to the inner, private sphere. Sharia law embraces the whole of human life, political as well as private, material as well as spiritual. The God disclosed in the Hebrew Scriptures is likewise concerned with the whole of human existence, a concern which is expressed in the Jewish Torah; and Christianity grew out of this soil. The papal encyclical *Immortale Dei* of Pope Leo XIII reads rather strangely today, but it is salutary to hear the words, for they remind us that we cannot draw an absolute line between historic Christianity and Islam in this respect. The encyclical said:

> It is a sin in the state not to have care of religion ... or out of the many forms of religion to adopt that one which chimes in with the fancy, for we are bound absolutely to worship God in that way in which He hath shown to be His will.

According to one authoritative Catholic source a few decades ago, 'no state is justified in supporting error or in according error the same recognition as truth', the truth referred to being embodied in the Catholic religion. The Roman Catholic Church now puts things in a much more nuanced way, but on certain issues, which are regarded as right or wrong by natural law, such as abortion, they would still hold that the state has an absolute duty to reject error, however people might vote. Leaving that particular issue aside, however, all Christians would now agree with John Locke's reasoning, that religious freedom is a requirement of genuine religion itself. Nevertheless, we still have to pay attention to the propensity of strongly held world-views, of which religion is one manifestation, to act intolerantly in practice, whatever they hold in theory. John Stuart Mill, after pointing out the argument of great thinkers in favour of religious tolerance, wrote:

Yet so natural to mankind is intolerance in whatever they really care about that religious freedom has hardly anywhere been practically realized, except where religious indifference, which dislikes to have its peace disturbed by theological quarrels, has added its weight to the scale. In the minds of almost all religious persons, even in the most tolerant countries, the duty of tolerance is admitted with tacit reserves ... Wherever the sentiment of the majority is still genuine and intense, it is found to have abated little of its claim to be obeyed.[2]

Before we sigh and groan that the problem, as correctly seen by Mill, seems even worse than we initially imagined it, there are two other points to note briefly.

First, although I am talking about religion, what I say can apply to any world-view, not just one based on a belief in the transcendent. Leaving aside Fascism, which had some pagan religious roots, the most intolerant movements of the twentieth century were Russian and Chinese Marxism and the Chinese Cultural Revolution. The numbers killed then in the desire to achieve ideological conformity were far greater than those in any religious persecutions of the same century.

Secondly, is our much-prized tolerance in the West really tolerance? Tolerance, said G. K. Chesterton, is the virtue of those who do not believe anything. Then there are the probing lines of W. B. Yeats in his poem 'The Second Coming':

The best lack all conviction, while the worst
Are full of passionate intensity.

A character in one of Graham Greene's novels says:

The church condemns violence, but it condemns indifference more harshly. Violence can be the expression of love, indifference never.[3]

These quotations bear out what Mill said, namely that one major factor bringing about tolerance has been the decline in intensity of belief. It poses very sharply the question as to whether there can be a form of tolerance that is not simply the expression of indifference and unbelief. Can there be a more deeply grounded tolerance, one which is in part the expression of a passionate intensity of belief, of profound conviction and love?

Although religious freedom is in some sense the most fundamental of all freedoms, there are many others that have been and continue to be crucial: freedom from slavery, feudalism, dictatorship, communism, colonialism, racism, economic imperialism, patriarchy, sexism and so on. Here as often as not we use the word 'liberty' to mean freedom from some crippling restraint which is not of our choosing. In this sense freedom has been one of the rallying cries of peoples and nations. *Cry Freedom* was the title of one well-known book at the time of Apartheid, as it was the great theme of Solidarity in the Cold War.

It should be noted at this stage that talk about freedom or liberty is more problematical than the language might suggest. For freedom can be a procedural freedom, as we might say that everyone is free to vote. But there is also the question of whether we have the freedom to realise our chosen goals, our capacity, or what Amartya Sen calls our capability. For Sen, simply measuring people's estimate of their own happiness is not enough. What is no less important are their capabilities, their ability to achieve what they choose. Sen's position on this had been well put some years ago from a Christian point of view by William Temple. He wrote:

> The first aim of social progress must be to give the fullest possible scope for the exercise of all powers and qualities which are distinctly personal: and of those the most fundamental is deliberate choice. Consequently, society must be so arranged as to give to every citizen the maximum opportunity for making deliberate choices and the best possible training for the use of that opportunity. Freedom must be freedom *for* something as well as freedom *from* something. It must be the actual ability to form and carry out a purpose.[4]

This, as we shall see, is not unrelated to the different ways in which we can also think about equality.

All these desired freedoms can be justified by the reason mentioned earlier. It belongs to our God-given dignity as human beings that we are free to live our lives without being forced into certain courses of action against our wills, and that we have the scope and opportunity to strive for what we choose. According to Luke, at the beginning of his ministry Jesus went into the synagogue at Nazareth and read a passage from the prophet Isaiah:

> The spirit of the Lord is upon me
> Because he has anointed me;
> He has sent me to announce good news to the poor,
> To proclaim release for prisoners
> And recovery of sight to the blind;
> To let the broken victims go free,
> To proclaim the year of the Lord's favour.

> Luke 4:18–19

Release and freedom are the keynotes of this passage and it is not surprising that liberation theology has been a major Christian perspective over the last 40 years. Now clearly, many of the expressions of the desire for freedom that I have mentioned could also be championed on the basis of other values – equality, for example, or a desire for human flourishing, and it is clear that, as we should expect, there is much overlap.

EQUALITY

There are of course many respects in which human beings are unequal. Most obviously, we are unequal in our natural endowments. Some people are intelligent, others less so; some are beautiful, some more ordinary; some are built to succeed at a particular sport, others are physically clumsy; some are gifted artistically, others with 'It', others in the ability to make good relationships. We need this variety of talents and abilities for society to function. What St Paul said about the body of Christ, that we need one another, is applicable to society as a whole (1 Cor. 12).

However, that said, we are equal in the most fundamental and important sense. For we are all of equal worth and dignity as human beings. No one human being is of less value as a human being than any other. For a Christian this is grounded in the fact that we are all equally created, cherished, and redeemed by the one God. You do not have to be a Christian to believe that all human beings are of equal worth. Many people of very different beliefs share that conviction. But the religious underpinning of this belief would be expected to strengthen it. In a family of orphans the children are conscious of belonging together and of every sibling being of value. In a family brought up by loving parents who, whilst recognising the different talents and interests of their children, value each of them equally, one would expect that sense of belonging together in an equality of worth to be even stronger. So here, as in other areas, a secular perspective and a Christian one are not mutually exclusive. Rather, there is much overlap, with, a Christian would say, some shared moral insight being enriched and deepened in a particular way by religious faith.[5]

The Christian Church, for all the inequalities that it has encouraged or tolerated in practice, has never lost sight of this most fundamental sense of all in which we are of equal worth and dignity in the eyes of God. It has always been quite clear that the rich are in danger of going to hell, and the poor have a good chance of going to heaven. The crucial question, though, is how far the Church has seen the implications of this Christian conviction in terms of public policy.

A good example is slavery. In the New Testament it is clear that a shared Christian faith radically transformed the relative status of the slave and owner. Both were on an equal footing in the eucharistic community and both were equally accountable to the one Master in heaven (Col. 4:1). However, it is equally the case that at that time the Church accepted the institution of slavery rather than questioning it, or seeking to live out the implications of its belief in human equality in the social order. However, the

Christian conviction of equality implanted some yeast which eventually started to change the whole body politic.

The struggle to end slavery was a long one and there is space to mention only two points. The first concerns Bartolomeo de las Casas. Las Casas arrived in what we call the West Indies in 1502. In 1511 another Dominican, Antonio de Montesinos, arrived on Hispaniola (today's Haiti and the Dominican Republic) and preached a sermon to the Spanish settlers who were trying to enslave the indigenous people. 'Are they not men? ... Are you not bound to love them as yourselves? In such a state as this, you can no more be saved than the Turks.' It is not difficult to imagine the fury this sermon aroused and the attempts which were made to get Montesinos silenced and expelled. Las Casas heard this sermon. The implications took some time to sink in, but when they did, he spent the whole of the rest of his life working against the enslavement of the indigenous people. The second example is the piece of pottery made for mass consumption by Wedgwood during the struggle against the African slave trade. It depicted a kneeling, shackled African reaching out his hands and pleading, 'Am not I a man like you?' The issue in the sixteenth century and in the nineteenth century was the recognition of other human beings as human beings, and therefore as those who were to be treated as such: as free citizens, not slaves.

This deep conviction about our fundamental equality has continued to ferment ever since the seventeenth century, Christian conviction joining forces with those who approach the issue from a progressive secular point of view. It has been worked out in terms of equal freedom to practise one's religion, as already mentioned, equality before the law and equality of political franchise.

The basis of modern democracy is that one counts for one. No pocket boroughs, no disenfranchised citizens, not one law for the powerful and one for the weak. The political implications of this were spelt out in the Putney Debates in the seventeenth century by Colonel Rainsborough:

I think the poorest he in England hath a life to live, as the greatest he. Therefore every man that is to live under a government, ought first, by his own consent to put himself under that government. The poorest man in England is not at all bound to a government that he hath not had a vote to put himself under.

The ferment of this conviction has continued to bring about change, as expressed, for example, in the American Civil Rights movement culminating, we could say, with the election of President Obama, or before that, with the ending of Apartheid in South Africa. It has been to the fore in recent legislation concerning gay and lesbian people. And it continues, for example, in the ongoing struggle to obtain true equality for women in the workplace, and in obtaining proper access for disabled people to all the goods and services of society. A new Equalities Bill is even now on its way through Parliament. So equality has been absolutely fundamental to the whole development of our civic and social existence as a society. My point is both that this is rightly a crucially important conviction and, with the utmost respect to secularists who champion it, that it is one that is deeply rooted in Christian faith, a faith which has played its fair share in ensuring that its implications are worked out in every aspect of society.

But have they been? And can they be? There is one area where there is still gross and growing inequality, and that is in the economic sphere. Why is this so? Here we go back to the triad of this chapter – liberty, equality and human community.

The movers behind the French Revolution of 1789 believed that *liberté, egalité, fraternité* went together, and that if you achieved one, the others would begin to follow. They thought that if only the old feudal inequalities were done away with, there would be equality, and from this there would flow genuine freedom of choice and true human community. The old order kept people in their place, and severely limited their choice. With choice opened up, it was assumed that everyone would prosper. In fact, as we know, this has happened to only a limited extent. Opening up choice for everyone has in fact led to inequalities of many different kinds, most obviously of course in the continuing divisions between the rich and poor as reflected so starkly in figures on health and mortality. Men living in certain parts of Glasgow have a life expectancy that is ten years less than people living in the south-east of England, and what is particularly shocking is that over the last 30 years this gap has widened, not narrowed.

One result of what has actually happened in the economic sphere is that today there is an assumption that choice and equality are essentially opposed to one another, and there has been a sharp polarisation between those advocating policies offering more choice and those who stress state action to achieve greater equality. However, I believe that it is a mistake to think that these values of choice and equality are always mutually incompatible. A market economy depends on the value of equality as well as on freedom of choice. For in stressing choice, we are stressing the fact that every individual consumer is equally free to choose. As Ronald Dworkin has put it, 'Under the special condition that people differ only in preferences for goods and activities, the market is more egalitarian than any alternative of comparable generality.'[6]

The qualifying clause is, however, crucially important. People do not differ only in their preferences. They differ hugely in the opportunities open to them to take advantage of those preferences. So while I think it is important not to see choice and equality as mutually conflicting values, we have always to bear in mind the context in which people make their choices. As one of the greatest of all theorists of equality, R. H. Tawney, once put it, 'The existence of such opportunities in fact, and not merely in form, depends, not only upon an open road, but upon an equal start.' Or again, 'Equality of opportunity is fictitious without equality in the circumstances under which men have to develop and exercise their capacities.'[7]

G. K. Chesterton once remarked that the average Englishman was less interested in the equality of man than he was in the inequality of racehorses. I am not sure that is still true, and whilst there is no great support for a flat notion of equality, people are offended by great and growing inequalities. In particular, at the moment there is a widespread sense of moral outrage against bankers who, whilst being responsible for the near financial collapse of the banking system, resulting in millions being dispossessed of their homes and losing their jobs, have safeguarded their obscene bonuses and pensions. Not least of the ill effects of such stark inequalities is that this leads to a failure to achieve true human community, the third of the three values championed by the French revolutionaries.

HUMAN COMMUNITY

The French Revolution saw fraternity as the great goal to be achieved in human society. That word can strike people as gender loaded today, and an alternative, sorority, as equally so – hence my use of the phrase 'human community'.

Since the Enlightenment there has been one consistent fallacy, shared by both secularists and Christians, and that is an over-individualistic understanding of what it is to be a human being. I accept that this has appeal. When this takes shape as libertarianism, it contains a powerful moral vision. Here, for example, is how Timothy Garton Ash puts it:

> Liberals start from liberalism. I'm a liberal, so I start from liberalism – not in the parody version propagated by the American right, but liberalism properly understood as a quest for the greatest possible measure of individual freedom, compatible with freedom for others.

The overriding value is as he puts it: 'the greatest possible measure of individual freedom'. The problem with this view, whether as stated by someone like Garton Ash, or proponents of the free market, is not that they have no doctrine of society, but that they have a very weak one, one which does not do justice to the essentially social nature of human beings. The view of at least some of those who emphasise individual freedom in this way is that society is like a criss-cross of well-used paths. Each individual

---

makes their own way, and the constant wear creates certain definite paths which they all eventually come to have in common.

But society is more than this. Mind is a social reality. We get talked into talking and doing that talking inside ourselves that we call thinking, through our relationships with other human persons. We are essentially inter-personal. We become persons in and through our relationships with other persons. So human community, first in the family and then in wider communities including the state, is not simply an add-on to our nature, but an essential aspect of it. One way in which this has been expressed is in the Catholic understanding of the state. This is not just seen as a result of and a remedy for the fall, but as something natural. It is natural for human beings to come together to share responsibility for the ordering of the common life.

The implication of this view is that the role of the government is not simply to maximise the liberty of its citizens; it is to act on behalf of the whole for the common good. This includes every aspect of policy, economic and social. This responsibility does not mean sitting light to the importance of individual freedom. On the contrary, it is part of the good of society as a whole, and not only for the individuals within it, that individual freedom should be respected. But this is not the only value and not in all cases the overriding one.

It was suggested above that the concepts of both liberty and equality are complex. They carry a variety of meanings, and at the same time the two concepts are not as opposed as some like to think. In reality most people will accept that both liberty, in some sense, and equality, in some sense are important, and that in practice when we are thinking about what is the right course of action we are unlikely to make one value of such importance that it overrides all others. Amartya Sen in *The Idea of Justice* particularly wishes to reject the idea of a unifocal approach. He discusses this not only in relation to the particular value of liberty, mentioned above, but in relation to his example of the three flute players that recurs throughout the book. There is only one flute, but three people who have a claim upon it. One person is a superb flautist and they would make best use of the flute. Another person is very deprived, and a flute would be the only possession they had which enabled them to enjoy themselves. A third person is the one who actually made the flute. To whom should the flute belong? Sen's argument is that a convincing rational case can be made out for all three, and it is not possible to have a unifocal perspective which rules out the other two. However, and this is another point he wishes to stress, this does not mean a state of moral paralysis. For whereas some philosophers in recent years have stressed the incommensurability of values, he argues that real differences do not in fact stop us making considered rational and moral judgements. Oranges and apples are indeed different, but that does not stop us choosing between them, perhaps a different choice on different occasions. So it is that when we are thinking of the needs of the most deprived people in the world, we can make a rational, moral decision about how best to help them, which will involve taking into account the kind of rational justification put forward by all three claimants to the flute, not just one.[8]

For those of a tidy mind, this rejection of a unifocal approach to justice can be frustrating. However, from a Christian point of view it has two great advantages. First, if it is God, and God alone, who is absolute, then we ought to be wary of placing any one principle, philosophical or political, in that position. The fact that we have to make a judgement in relation to a number of different moral considerations, taking them all into account, is a feature of being a finite, limited being. Secondly, Sen's approach is to prioritise the voices of the marginalised, and to let them be heard in the political debate. He rejects a purely theoretical approach to justice, as in the theory of John Rawls, and argues that justice is about taking everyone into account, especially the powerless, in continuing rational public debate about how the range of human needs can be met. This again accords wonderfully well with a Christian understanding of what it means to be part of the human community as a whole. It also chimes in with the practice of the best aid agencies, like Christian Aid, who like to work in and through partners in the countries that need help, so that the needs responded to are the needs stated by those who are needy. In terms of the picture of the three claimants to the one flute, those who are seeking help will be in the best position at any one time to set the priorities.

Another very interesting approach to issues of justice and human community has just come from the 2009 Reith Lecturer, Michael Sandel.[9] Like Sen, he takes John Rawls very seriously and believes he has put forward the most convincing case for equality that we have yet had. As mentioned in the previous chapter, John Rawls is famous for posing the question about what political principles we would choose if none of us knew what position, or what advantages or disadvantages, we would have when we were born. We have to devise a society 'under a veil of ignorance' about whether we would be a slave or a millionaire. On the basis of a 'hypothetical consent', he argues that first, we would all agree that we would want the basic freedoms we now subscribe to, and secondly, whilst recognising that some people would be born into wealth and others into poverty, such inequalities would only be justified in so far as they helped the poorest and most vulnerable members of society. If we all got together, before we were born, to agree on some basic principles, he argues that these two are the only ones to which everyone would consent. Whilst Sandel, like Sen, goes some of the way with Rawls, he argues in relation to this and all modern political philosophies that they try to dodge the question about the nature of the good, and the good life. In a series of vivid examples, he shows that we cannot in fact do this. We cannot just leave people to choose their own lifestyle, or leave the market to its own momentum. Both social libertarianism and market libertarianism leave unanswered questions. For issues of value and fairness keep obtruding themselves, and that raises the question of what we as a society regard as good. Like Sen, he acknowledges that there will be no immediate agreement about this – hence the appeal of libertarian views which leave it to the individual – but in fact what we need to do is engage with one another concerning the nature of the common good of society.

The New Testament sets out a vision of the Christian community as a sign of true society. For it is humanity reconstituted round

Jesus, and as such is a new humanity, both a sign and a pledge of what is coming to be. This community is one that is grounded in and motivated by love. Of course, it has its manifest failures. But you cannot read the letters of St Paul without grasping the true nature of the Church as a community of mutual giving and receiving. It is a community of different gifts and talents in which all are equally valued in making a contribution to the harmonious working of the whole body, the body of Christ.

In society as a whole, however, people are held together not just by love but by coercion. Love alone is not enough. Sadly, we need the police and armies. The tension this involves in applying the ethical teaching of Jesus to society as a whole is apparent in a number of areas, but here my theme is the relationship between the Church as true human community and the wider society in which it is set. I have already said it is meant to be a sign of true society and a pledge of what humanity under God will one day come to be. But meanwhile it is also meant to be transformative of that wider society in its public as well as its individual dimension. This means that individual Christians should care about the transformation of the wider society in which they are set in all its aspects, not least in its political structures, institutions and policies. This is one of the ways in which the community of the Kingdom of God taught by Jesus bears upon the world, keeping us alert to impossible possibilities.

One good example of the way this works is the principle of taxation. Because we are what we are, it is necessary to have a policy of taxation enforced by law. If people refuse to pay their taxes they can go to jail. But from the standpoint of the community of the Kingdom, taxes are a sign of a society that lives by mutual giving and receiving. They are not just about paying our fair share of the cost of the roads, the police and the army. They express love. Take the position of people who are severely disabled, who cannot work and who have no support, financial or otherwise. In our best moments we would like to help them ourselves. But because it is not practical simply to leave their support to individual initiative and because we do not always or even usually act on what we might decide to do in our best moments, we agree that such people should be supported by the state, paid for through taxation. Seen in that way, the taxes are an expression of self-knowledge, realism and loving concern. They are a sign of the Kingdom making a difference in the world as we know it.

Some theologians today, as in the past, have wanted to see the Christian community set apart from wider society with its own distinctive life and values which it brings to bear on that wider society only in radical difference and challenge. But in fact the Christian community and wider society, at least in the West, are much more closely bound up than that view would suggest and the boundaries between them are much harder to delineate. What this means in reality is that the progressive changes that have taken place since the Enlightenment have been the result of action by both Christians and secularists. That is still the case today on a range of issues. It also means that the Christian community itself is still very much like the field of wheat and tares growing together that is suggested by one of the parables of Jesus (Matt. 13:24–30).

Christians therefore will properly support the role of government in acting for the common good, even sometimes when it limits individual choice. This has two major implications, one in social policy and the other in economic policy.

The modern libertarian view is that each individual has their own moral standards, and provided this does not lead them to harming others, they should be left free to do what they want. This will result in a virtually total absence of censorship and the minimum of regulation. A good example is the view of Simon Jenkins that women should be free to sell their eggs for what they can get for them and men should similarly be free to sell their sperm, both activities being forbidden by the Human Fertilization and Embryology Authority at the moment.[10]

In contrast to this libertarian view, it can be pointed out, as already argued, that we are social beings and it is right that the government should be concerned for the common good. Furthermore, that common good will, as the term implies, have a moral dimension. Nothing in this life is morally neutral, certainly not the state. All its institutions will embody certain values, and these will be the result of that society's history and culture: and that history and culture will have been significantly shaped by its religion. Those values can and ought always to be questioned. Furthermore, some societies, whose history has left a legacy of some barbaric practices based on twisted values, must be radically changed. But nevertheless, every society will quite rightly reflect a set of values and standards which may rightly reflect many of the values and standards of its individual members, but which also stands apart from them with an independent validity. There is, however, a crucially important qualification, which is that in our society respect for individual freedom is a major value of our society itself. It will only be overridden with very good cause.

The other areas where the common good is a highly relevant value are in relation to economic and social policies. In a competitive world, and a highly competitive market economy, those most likely to succeed are those with resources behind them and who know how to make the system work to their own advantage. A market economy may be the most efficient way of ensuring the prosperity of everyone in the society, but it is inevitable that there will be those who lose out through no fault of their own; those who do not have the capacity to benefit from the system; those whom market forces drive to the wall. If government has a responsibility for the common good, this must include a responsibility for the well-being of such people. In short, it has a responsibility not just to enable the market to work, but to help people participate in it and make their way in it; and also to ensure that those who are genuinely incapable of doing so are properly supported.

This value of the common good understood in these inclusive terms is reaffirmed and undergirded by the concern which the New Testament urges Christians to have for the poor. Furthermore, in judging the rightness or wrongness of particular policies, this will mean asking as a matter of priority what their effect is going to be on the most vulnerable members of society. There needs to be a proper Christian solidarity with the marginalised, which asks questions about the effects of all national and international economic and political policies on them.[11]

In America the richest 1 per cent of the population own more than the combined wealth of the bottom 90 per cent of American families, with, as we know, some 40 million people lacking any basic health care. In 1980 the Chief Executive Officers of major US corporations were paid 42 times what their workers earned. In 2007 they were paid 344 times the pay of the average worker. India now produces 2 million graduates a year and half the world's software engineers, but nearly half of the women in the country remain illiterate. You do not need to have what W. B. Yeats called a 'levelling, rancorous, rational sort of mind' to worry about the effect of this on human solidarity, our sense of belonging together in one human community.

As mentioned earlier, when the revolutionaries in France first coined the slogan, 'Liberty, Equality, Fraternity' (or, as we would say today, human community), they thought that if only the old, hierarchical inequalities were done away with and people were genuinely free to make their way in the world, this would bring about that much-desired human community. Just the opposite has happened. Vast bonuses may or may not bring financial benefit all round, but what is their wider effect if the mass of people are filled with a sense of moral outrage? David Hare's play *The Power of Yes* is an analysis of the cause of the near collapse of the West's financial system. At the end the financier George Soros recalls a conversation with Alan Greenspan. Greenspan had said, 'The benefits of the market are so great that you have to live with the price.' To this Soros had replied, 'Yes, but Alan, the people who end up paying the price are never the people who get the benefits.'[12]

Both liberty and equality are values that are deeply rooted in the Bible and the Christian view of what it is to be a human being, but they cannot be seen apart from the goal of true human community.

DOES GOD BELIEVE IN HUMAN RIGHTS?

HUMAN ROOTS AND RELIGIOUS FAITH

The drive to get human rights acknowledged in theory and observed in practice is one of the great movements of our time. When future historians look back, they will single out the 1948 United Nations Declaration of Human Rights and what has followed from it, as one of the outstanding achievements of our age. Alas, there are still terrible violations of human rights in many countries and too often only lip service is paid to the idea. Nevertheless, there is now an internationally agreed benchmark for how individuals should be treated that had never been there before.

Although the movement to get internationally agreed statements about human rights was very much a product of World War II, the theoretical discussion about the nature of rights and their basis is usually thought of as going back to the seventeenth century. What about before that time? Was the idea of rights invented then, or did it have roots going back into classical times?

It is true that the language of rights was not so much in evidence before the seventeenth century. Nevertheless, what rights are trying to safeguard was expressed in other ways, most obviously in the concepts of law and of justice. The law that forbids stealing carries with it the idea that people have a right to their own property. Similarly, the law that forbids us to harm other people carries with it the idea that people have a right not to be gratuitously hurt. Or to put it in the language of morality rather than law: if I have a duty to respect the person and property of someone else, they have a right to live their life without attacks on them. In personal terms, I have a responsibility to respect them and they have a right to be so respected. So the idea of rights is built into the very notion of law. However, in the modern world we are talking not just about legal rights but about human rights. These are about what is due to us by virtue of our very humanity. These human rights will usually be expressed in law and they need to be so expressed in order to be fully effective. But the point about human rights language is that it implies a moral basis for those laws, and it acts as a catalyst both to have such human rights enshrined in law and to go on working for the extension or improvement of such laws in order to conform more nearly to the moral imperative.[1] This moral imperative also has its roots in our classical and Christian past in the notion of natural law. This is the idea that our moral awareness, our capacity for making morally based decisions, belongs to our very nature as human beings, whatever our religious beliefs. As indicated earlier in the chapter on law and morality, philosophically this has been a much-disputed notion in the modern world; and in its Roman Catholic form, where it seems to be suggested that you can almost read off the content of natural law by looking at the course of nature, as in ordinary sexual intercourse, it seems to be untenable. But I would still maintain that there is a moral law and that all human beings by virtue of being human have some capacity for distinguishing right from wrong and acting morally. It used to be argued that this cannot be the case because there are such different understandings of what is right and wrong between different cultures. But although there are some differences, recent studies show there is much more in common.[2]

From a Christian point of view the concept of a natural law has been rejected by some Protestant thinkers as failing to take seriously the fact of the fall and its consequence that we are born in original sin. However, St Paul is quite clear that all people do have some capacity for moral insight and moral behaviour. Their own thoughts argue the case, sometimes against them and sometimes even for them, with their inner conscience as the touchstone (Rom. 2:14–15).

This means that if morality is natural to humanity, there is that in us which is capable of making laws that reflect that morality, and which continues to seek ways of improving those laws in order to try to ensure that they do so more adequately. That natural law, to retain the old phrase for a moment, will help shape our ideas as to how we should behave in relation to our fellow human beings and has taken effect in international human rights legislation.

So, crucial as it is to obtain legal recognition of rights, their basis is not in law itself but in prior ethical considerations. This fact is important in several ways. The Universal Declaration of Human Rights adopted by the UN in 1948 does not have the status of a legal treaty but it is nevertheless regarded as an authoritative articulation of universal human rights which has had significant effect in bringing about such laws and covenants. The fact that human rights are rooted in ethics means that there have been and continue to be protests when they are violated, even when a country has no specific law in relation to rights. It leads to agitation to change unjust laws. It leads to movements to challenge old assumptions, as with the beginning of the women's rights movement in the work of Mary Wolstonecraft in the eighteenth century. In short, the ethical recognition of universal human rights is a continuing dynamic to enact laws which enshrine them and which shift us in the direction of a more just world.

So, the concept of human rights grows out of a long tradition of classical Christian thinking about morally based law which relates to all human beings by virtue of their humanity. In the pre-modern period it took effect in such declarations as that of the Magna Carta in 1215, which guaranteed barons, and by extension, all freemen, certain legal rights, notably the right to appeal against unjust imprisonment. Nevertheless, the language of rights and its modern emphasis only really came to the fore in the seventeenth century and took decisive political form in the following one. The American Declaration of Independence of 1776 stated:

> All men are created equal and are endowed by their Creator with certain inalienable rights.

It is important to note that they believed that these rights had been endowed by their Creator. This reflected the fact that most of the founding fathers were people of religious faith, and their understanding of what we owe to one another as human beings was seen and stated in that perspective. Some of them, like Thomas Jefferson, the main architect of the declaration, were Deists, rather than Christians, and most of those behind the 1789 declaration in France were indeed Deists. But still, it is important to note this religious reference, and the fact that even the French declaration was made 'in the presence and under the auspices of the Supreme Being'.

Roger Rushton, after an examination of the thought of Aquinas, the sixteenth-century Spanish theologians and John Locke, rightly concludes:

> So the apparently secular discourse of human rights, far from being something alien imposed on religious life from outside, has grown from within a religious tradition in response to its deepest insights into God's creative presence in the World.[3]

Despite these very clear affirmations of religious motivation and justification, there is a widespread suspicion or even assumption that the modern human rights movement is really a secular one and human rights have a secular rather than a religious foundation. Let us look at some of these suspicions. It is said, for example, that Christianity is primarily concerned with responsibilities and duties rather than rights. Now it is true that responsibilities and rights do not always go neatly together. I have a responsibility not to be cruel to animals, whether or not animals have rights, which is a disputed concept. And no one should underestimate the importance of the concept of responsibility. However, as mentioned above, in law responsibilities also imply rights, as rights imply responsibilities. They are held together in law, which is there to ensure both that we act responsibly towards our neighbour and that our neighbour is left free to act within his or her rights. Some argue that duties precede rights and the latter flow from the former; others argue that rights come first, and duties arise out of a recognition of these rights.[4]

Closely linked to this suspicion of rights by some Christians is the feeling that it is somehow selfish to talk about rights. People criticise what they call an increasing sense of entitlement, for this seems contrary to the Christian faith, which discourages claiming things for oneself. However, rights are more often than not trying to ensure that other people are properly respected. It is not selfish to try to ensure that the most marginalised or oppressed are able to lead a properly human life. It is not selfish to try to obtain the release of people who have been imprisoned by an oppressive regime for expressing their views or who are in danger of being tortured. At the time of the Peasants' Revolt, Martin Luther said to them, 'Suffering, suffering, cross, cross. This and nothing else is the Christian law.' But whilst that might have been an understanding of how he himself should respond to injustice, it was not his place to tell others who were suffering that they should put up with it rather than fight to oppose it. There are indeed texts in the New Testament that tell us that Christian discipleship involves accepting unjust suffering rather than resisting it. But that is a matter of personal discipleship. It cannot be used as the basis for opposing the establishment of a just society in which everyone's rights are properly recognised and observed.

Furthermore, it can be questioned whether it is indeed right, even as a matter of personal discipleship, for people always simply to put up with injustice. One of the reasons why women have been so badly treated down the ages is that they have been encouraged to be submissive rather than stand up for themselves. This has been very damaging for their sense of their own worth and dignity. It may be that we owe it to ourselves before God to stand up for ourselves, and to assert ourselves against all that would subjugate and humiliate us.

D. H. Lawrence once wrote a poem parodying a famous hymn:

> Stand up, but not for Jesus!
> It's a little late for that.
> Stand up for justice and a jolly life.
> I'll hold your hat.

Stand up, stand up for justice,
ye swindled little blokes!
Stand up and do some punching,
give 'em a few hard pokes.
Stand up for jolly justice
you haven't got much to lose:
a job you don't like and a scanty chance
for a dreary little booze.
Stand up for something different,
and have a little fun
fighting for something worth fighting for
before you've done.
Stand up for a new arrangement
for a chance of life all round
for freedom, and the fun of living
bust in, and hold the ground![5]

In that poem, he brings out well, in popular form, the political, moral and psychological liberation that is necessary from certain forms of Christianity. But it was of course written before the advent of the feminist movement and the emphasis is upon 'swindled little blokes' rather than women. But its spirit applies even more to those countless women round the world who have been and still are the subject of violence, both physical and psychological.

THE MORAL BASIS OF HUMAN RIGHTS

Various philosophical arguments have been put forward as the basis for a belief in human rights. My own view is closely related to Ronald Dworkin's:

> Anyone who professes to take rights seriously must accept, at the minimum, the vague but powerful idea of human dignity.[6]

Similarly Amartya Sen finds the basis of human rights 'in the ethical principle that every individual has claims to the attention and regard of others.'[7]

Philosophical arguments seek to provide a firm rational basis for the recognition of this ethical claim upon us. One of them, rule utilitarianism, is discussed briefly below. But if we accept that the basis of human rights is the recognition of human dignity and the claim to regard, as do Dworkin and Sen, then there is a rather different relationship between human rights and the reasons that might be given for believing in them. For there are some judgements we make where the reasons we put forward are not proofs leading inescapably to a particular conclusion but reasons to indicate why there has been a particular act of recognition and response in the first place. The situation is closely parallel to the kind of discussion we might have about a relationship. For example, if someone asks us what we see in a particular friend, we will outline qualities or characteristics which we recognise in them. What we say will be indicative reasons; reasons which indicate why the friend is a friend with the assumption that the person to whom they are told will, as a result of what is said, see similar qualities in the person, and come to appreciate them. There is no guarantee that this will happen. It is possible to go on giving reason after reason, with the other person still unconvinced. But the reasons have done their work when they do indeed see what you see. There is an act of recognition with an appropriate response.

There are parallels to this when we are asked to say why we judge a piece of literature or work of art highly. It is good to be able to give convincing reasons if we are asked to do so, but those reasons will never amount to a proof with inescapable logic.

We could even go beyond this and say that in relationships the best reason is that there is no reason. When I first knew my wife, her father had given her a brand-new, beautiful, light-blue MGA, one of the nicest sports cars ever made. She would not have liked it if she thought I had married her for the car! She might have been more pleased if I said that it was because of her beauty, but even then, she might have come back to me in the words of the Beatle song and said, 'Well, what about when I'm wrinkled and grey?' In the end people want to be loved for themselves, because they are themselves, and reasons given can detract from that. C. S. Lewis, writing about the pleasures of appreciation, said: 'Something has not merely gratified our sense in fact but claimed our appreciation by right.' If that is true of aesthetic appreciation, it is even more true of the process through which we appreciate the worth of a human being. This is not just a matter of feeling, but the sense that something has 'claimed our appreciation by right'.

This is well brought out by the Irish writer, Frank McGuiness, in *There came a gypsy riding by*. In this play a family meet together on the anniversary of their son Gene's suicide. They are given a note he wrote indicating no reason at all as to why he had taken his own life. They are doubly distressed: for his death, and the fact that he gave no reason for it. Then the father says to his wife:

> I looked into his coffin the morning of his funeral. I said something to him that nobody heard. I've not told you nor Simon nor Louise … I told him if I were given one wish, I would go back in time to before he was born and I would not change him, Gene, I would still choose him. I would not change my child, no matter what.[8]

That is a fundamental act of appreciation, of someone being loved, of worth and of value, simply as they are for themselves. Reasons might elucidate that, but they cannot guarantee to bring it about.

We should therefore expect what is in fact the case, that people who have little capacity for formal reasoning can and do make heroic decisions. Perhaps they have been nurtured in a family imbued with a deep respect for all other human beings. This becomes part of their very being. They instinctively behave in this way to others. That they do this seems to us admirable. It is more important than being able to give reasons for such behaviour. Some of the most moving stories to come out of World War II are those where simple, unlettered people, perhaps farm lads or labourers, simply refused to go along with the Nazis or sheltered Jews, usually at the cost of their own lives, and this they did not with any overt philosophical or religious justification in mind, but for its own sake. A similar point was made by Montaigne in his essay on friendship:

Does God Believe in Human Rights?

If a man urge me to tell him wherefore I love him, I feel it cannot be expressed but by answering, because it was he, because it was myself ... it is not one especial consideration, nor two, nor three, nor four, nor a thousand. It is I wot not what kind of quintessence of all this commixture which seized my will.

Commenting on this, Margaret Macdonald has written:

Yet it is also correct to say that our decisions about worth are not merely arbitrary, and intelligent choices are not random. They cannot be proved correct by evidence. Nor, I suggest, do we try to prove them. What we do is to support and defend our decisions. The relation of the record of a decision to the considerations which support it is not that of proof to conclusion. It is much more like the defence of his client by a good counsel.[9]

All this has a very direct bearing on the issue of human rights and their foundation. For as suggested above, they are rooted in a recognition of the dignity and worth of every single human being, and the consequent response to that recognition. We may be able to give reasons for this recognition and we might use them to help other people see what we do, but the act of recognition is prior. Sometimes, as mentioned in the previous chapter, this comes with the force of a conversion experience, as when Bartolomeo de las Casas in the sixteenth century realised that the indigenous people who were being pressed into forced labour or even slavery, were human beings like himself, and as such were entitled to be treated as human. A similar conviction gripped the opponents of the slave trade and drove the American Civil Rights Movement.

Dworkin, in the quotation above, goes on to associate the idea of human dignity with Kant. One wonders why Kant is singled out rather than the framework of the Old Testament's legal codes, or Jesus, or Aquinas, to suggest just a few examples of pre-Kantian alternatives. The worth and dignity of the individual person is basic to Jewish, Christian and Muslim traditions. For according to these perspectives, we are made in the divine image, endowed with rationality and choice, able to think and choose and love and pray.

GOD RECOGNISES AND AFFIRMS THE VALUE OF HIS CREATION

This said, there is still a further suspicion about human rights; perhaps an even more fundamental one. Does God himself believe in human rights? There are some terrible stories in the Bible in which God is depicted as behaving in ways worse than the worst human tyrants, destroying whole peoples without a care for the innocent. Even if we reject these stories and say that they reflect an early stage of human thinking about the Divine, we have St Paul's analogy in which he compares human beings to clay in the hands of a potter:

> You will say, 'Then why does God find fault, if no one can resist his will?' Who do you think you are to answer God back? Can the pot say to the potter, 'Why did you make me like this?'? Surely the potter can do what he likes with the clay. Is he not free to make two vessels out of the same lump, one to be treasured, the other for common use?

> Romans 9:19–21

The fact is, however, we are not lumps of clay. We are clay that has been breathed into to give us minds and spirits. We can answer back. Like Job, we can insist on answering back and refusing all false piety. It is only tyrants who kill people for so doing. I do not believe that the God and Father of our Lord Jesus Christ is like that.

God has indeed made us. But that does not mean, as Paul suggested, that he can do what he likes with us.

It is well known that when Winston Churchill had his portrait painted by Graham Sutherland, he so disliked the result that he destroyed it. No doubt he took the view that he had paid for it, he owned it, and he could do what he liked with it. But suppose it was not a new portrait but a picture of one of his ancestors, say painted by Titian, for which he had always had an obsessive hatred, and which he destroyed? Was he really right to think that just because he owned it, he could do what he liked with it? Many would say that the painting was of great value, not just monetary value, and he had no right to destroy it. Ownership did not give him that right. So today, we tend to have strict planning laws about what people may or may not do with what they own, particularly if heritage is involved. We put preservation orders on trees and buildings and so on. Ownership does not confer an absolute right.

In his first treatise on government Locke criticises arguments in favour of absolute government. One of Locke's points is that parents do not have absolute rights over their children. There are various reasons for this, but one of them is that fathers do not actually create their children, only God does. As Locke says:

> To give life to that which has yet no being, is to frame and make a living creature, fashion the parts, and mould and suit them to their uses; and having proportioned and fitted them together, to put into them a living soul. He that could do this, might indeed have some pretence to destroy his own workmanship. But is there any one so bold that dares thus far arrogate to himself the incomprehensible works of the Almighty?[10]

What interests me in this sentence is the hesitant, qualified way in which Locke talks about what God might be entitled to do: 'He that could do this, might indeed have some pretence to destroy his own workmanship.' It is a *might* – it is not argued through that he *does* have such a right.

In fact I would suggest that the language of rights is totally out of place in such a consideration. God creates us and we are of such value to him that he comes amongst us in his own Son to seek us out and save us from ourselves, that we might live with him for ever. We are of unique worth in the eyes of God, and this is not because God just happens to regard us as of worth; the fact is that he has created us in his image, has bestowed on us that worth, which he then recognises. We are of worth in ourselves for ourselves, and God affirms this. The question of a right to destroy what he has made simply does not arise, whatever impression the Bible might sometimes give. Contra St Paul, we are not pots with which the potter may do what he wants. We are human beings whose value God rejoices in.

At the heart of Locke's religious view is that we are God's workmanship. Perhaps he particularly had in mind Ephesians 2:10, which says we are God's *poiema* or 'workmanship', in the old translation. But I particularly like the modern translation of this: 'we are God's work of art'.

The implications of this for the issue of human rights is that their basis is the inherent worth and dignity of each human being. From a Christian point of view this is rooted and grounded in our being of worth to God. But that worth can of course be seen and affirmed whether or not people share that belief. It is this belief in the dignity and worth of every human being in the body politic that is the basis of human rights. From a Christian perspective this is rooted in God's creation of us as free, and his total respect for that freedom, and his equal valuing of each of us. There is a Christian foundation if we will see it. But we can and do recognise those values even without the foundation.

OUR INCLINATION TO INJUSTICE MAKES LEGAL FORM NECESSARY

The basis of human rights is the dignity and value of every human being. But not this alone. In a family that is working normally there is no talk of rights. The members of the family naturally and instinctively take the others into account. Of course there are quarrels and disagreements. But these are not usually settled by appeal to 'my rights'. They are settled by argument and compromise. The language of rights enters in when the dignity of human beings is likely to be violated and they need to be protected in some way. It is because the world is full of injustice and cruelty, violence and discrimination, that such steps need to be taken. In short, the basis of rights is not just the dignity and worth of human

Does God Believe in Human Rights?

beings but the fact that we live in a world where this is daily denied and violated, and therefore the worth of human beings has to be enshrined and protected in law.

In fact this has always been the basis of law. If human beings were perfect there would be no need for law, at least in its coercive aspects. What is different about human rights law, however, is that it seeks to protect individuals not only from the cruelty of other individuals, but against potential state abuse. For although the state is the great upholder of laws which stop its citizens tearing one another apart, and which enable them to live with a degree of order and justice, the state itself is not neutral. It reflects the interests of its ruler, ruling class or interest groups. So, as mentioned above, the history of human rights is often seen as closely linked to the struggle for democracy and begins with Magna Carta in 1215 when the barons secured certain rights both for themselves and citizens more generally, against the king, at that time the embodiment of the state. The history continues with the charter of 1354 when Edward III introduced the important principle of due process of law. After the Civil War in the seventeenth century there was a gradual extension of the idea of the right to religious freedom and in the nineteenth and twentieth centuries, the right of everyone to participate fully in the political process. This is a struggle to secure fundamental rights and freedoms for everyone, whatever the government in power.

It might be thought that with the advent of liberal democracy the need to safeguard such rights would no longer be an issue. On the contrary, as Alexis de Tocqueville pointed out, there is always the possibility of the despotism or tyranny of the majority. Democratic government is in practice rule by the majority as measured by some particular system. But that rule needs safeguards in the same way as any other rule.

The majority have interests that will in some respects be different from the minorities which form the rest of the population. That is inevitable in a democracy. But it does mean that the fundamental rights and freedoms of those minorities must be protected. Beyond this, however, a government may have policies which do indeed seek to protect the vast majority of citizens and which have their support, but which in some way are seriously harmful to a few individuals. It is here that human rights really begin to bite. It is this which makes Ronald Dworkin's description of human rights as 'political trumps' so apt. As he has written:

> Individual rights are political trumps held by individuals. Individuals have rights when for some reason a collective good is not sufficient justification for denying them what they wish as individuals to have or do, or not a sufficient justification for imposing some loss or injury upon them.[11]

If someone has a right to something, then it is wrong for the government to deny it to him or her, even though it would be in the general interest to do so. The individual holds a trump card. This is a crucially important point. We see its relevance most clearly in the example of torture. A country in a state of emergency, or engaged in what President Bush called 'a war on terror', decides that the most effective way of gaining valuable information from suspected terrorists is by torturing them – let us say, using the notorious 'water-boarding' techniques practised under the Bush administration in America. There may be a very plausible reason for this in terms of national security. It is certainly in the interests of all citizens that they should be saved from attacks. But if there are human rights in place, all these reasons are to no avail in justifying torture. Human rights, by their very nature, override all such utilitarian reasons.

A good example of what is at issue occurred when Tony Blair seemed to suggest that he wanted to rebalance the relationship between the rights of suspected terrorists and the right of the community for security. As he said, 'The demands of the majority of the law-abiding community have to take precedence.' But this idea that it is a cost–benefit matter is a deeply misleading metaphor. Cost–benefit analysis is an important form of reasoning for most public policy issues, but not in the case of human rights. As Ronald Dworkin wrote about that view of Tony Blair:

This amazing statement undermines the whole point of recognizing human rights; it is tantamount to saying that there are no such things.[12]

This example returns us again, in a very sharp way, to the question about the underlying philosophical justification of human rights. For if we take a straightforward utilitarian position, that we should act in such a way as to promote the greatest good of the greatest number, then it could be argued that torture can be justified. The safety and security of the population as a whole would seem to be a greater good than the pain of a few individuals. It was no doubt for such reasons that the early utilitarians regarded human rights as nonsense on stilts. There are other more sophisticated forms of utilitarian reasoning. One is to justify the very moral principles on which a society is based on utilitarian grounds. This does not consider the effect of an individual acting or not acting in a particular way. It considers the effects of having or not having certain rules. For example, we might argue that a society that has certain morally based laws, like a prohibition of torture, will in the long run be a greater good than ones that do not. There is much to be said for this argument. For the fact is that in history the most terrible things have been justified by rulers on the basis of the first kind of utilitarian reasoning. No doubt Hitler justified trying to exterminate the Jews on the grounds that this would be beneficial to society. Stalin justified the state farms and gulags again on the grounds that these were in the interests of the society. So once we allow that kind of reasoning, there is the possibility of slippage into the justification of the most terrible policies. But the second kind of utilitarian thinking, a rule-based utilitarianism, aware of this, argues that it is in the interests of the greatest number that we have rules that never allow torture, even if a government at a particular time tries to make out an argument for it on utilitarian grounds.

Even a rule-based utilitarianism, however, does not seem to get at the heart of the matter. This is that our society is based on certain values. Because of the unique dignity and worth of every individual, we might say that my moral vision of society is one in which people should not be tortured whatever the circumstances. So we say, I want my society to be like that, whatever the consequences. That is what we stand for. That is what I stand for. This is what makes our society different from one which advocates terrorism, and I am not going to let them win a victory by making me act in a similar way.

Paradoxically, one of the contexts in which this kind of thinking is still very strong is in the services. I remember when I was in the Army a friend might say, 'Grenadiers don't behave like that.' Obviously this kind of thinking is closely linked to codes of honour. They depend not so much on any philosophical idea but upon creating a community with a particular kind of ethos. It can have powerful effects in the most difficult situations, as when a soldier refuses to gratuitously hurt a prisoner he has captured, simply on the grounds that his regiment 'does not do that kind of thing'. This approach to the issue is very close to 'virtue ethics', which has been to the fore in thinking about these issues in recent years. Virtue ethics does not answer all the questions we have in these difficult areas; in particular, it does not offer any help on how we resolve a difficult ethical dilemma. But in its emphasis on creating communities whose ethos is such as to encourage and build up certain virtues, it is clearly of great practical importance. For if people have been nurtured in communities which shape them into people of honesty, courage and selflessness, then in facing moral dilemmas, they are less likely to be swayed by what might otherwise seem the easy option.

ECONOMIC, SOCIAL AND CULTURAL RIGHTS

The great human rights movement began after World War II when, in the light of the terrible history of the previous two decades, there was an international mood to take steps to try to stop what happened in Nazi Germany or Russia happening again. Even more than before, it was obvious that individuals needed to be protected not just from other dangerous individuals but from the state itself. This movement, especially all the negotiation that was necessary to bring about the UN Declaration in 1948, was significantly the work of Christians. Not only were some of the main architects in Europe Christians themselves, but also leading figures in the World Council of Churches were a major influence.[13]

The original emphasis, for the reasons suggested above, was on securing civil and political rights. So the 1948 Declaration on Human Rights was spelled out in further detail on this in the International Covenant on Civil and Political Rights, adopted in 1966. In the same year, however, the International Covenant on Economic, Social and Cultural Rights was adopted. These two areas of human rights are rather different. For a society can and ought to sign up to the first, whatever its state of economic development. The second, however, clearly depends for its proper implementation on what is possible, and that depends on its stage of economic development. However, it is important to have the Covenant on Economic, Social and Cultural Rights as a benchmark which gives a moral imperative to move in the direction of its full implementation. It is tempting to say that the Covenant on Civil and Political Rights is the more fundamental of the two, for this can and ought to be observed now, whereas the other inevitably has an aspirational element in it. However, this would be a mistake. Indeed there are societies which have and do regard the second as more fundamental than the first. In particular, the old Soviet Union was very critical of the Western emphasis on political rights, regarding it as an expression of bourgeois individualism. They argued that people's right to have food, housing and work was even more fundamental and it was the state's prime obligation to ensure these, even if it meant sitting light to political rights. China today has a similar approach.

As was mentioned in a previous chapter, there is an excessive individualism in much Western political philosophy. From a Christian point of view, we are always persons in community, and the community cannot just be seen in terms of every individual doing his or her own thing. But the old Communist emphasis had a major distortion in it, for it failed to take into account the human will to power, and the need for this to be checked and balanced by countervailing powers. In particular, the power of government needs these checks and balances, with the ultimate sanction of allowing the population a free vote to choose a different government, as was discussed in the chapter on democracy. Here the point is that safeguarding individual rights against a misuse of state power is crucial. But because we are social beings, the state does also have a proper responsibility to ensure to the best of its ability that the basic requirements set out in the International Covenant on Economic, Social and Cultural Rights are met.[14]

This has been a particular emphasis of liberation theologians. José Bonino, for example, has written:

> For the vast majority of the population of the world today, the basic human right is the right to human life, to a human life. The deeper meaning of the violation of formal human rights is the struggle to vindicate these larger masses who claim their right to the means of life. The drive towards universality and the quest of the American and French Revolutions; the aspirations in the UN Declaration finds its historical focus today for us in the struggle of the poor, the economically and socially oppressed for their liberation.[15]

This means that human rights are not just negative – protecting individuals from harm, crucial though this is – but positive. The positive impulse is a continuing historical drive to ensure a reasonable standard of living, education and health care, all of which are today denied to so many millions in the world.

It has rightly been said that 'The modern human rights movement has been and continues to be, an astonishing moral phenomenon.'[16] This is to be celebrated. But there is still a huge way to go both to protect human beings from violations of their political rights in so many countries in the world and to ensure that their economic, social and cultural rights are guaranteed.

WHO DO WE THINK WE ARE? NATIONAL AND RELIGIOUS IDENTITIES

MULTIPLE IDENTITIES

In an interview Norman Tebbitt once said:

> A large proportion of Britain's Asian population fail to pass the cricket test. Which side do they cheer for? It's an interesting test. Are you still harking back to where you came from or where you are?

This remark highlights an issue that has been with us for some decades now, and is of growing importance. Where do our loyalties lie? It is not of course a new question. After Tebbitt's remark a cartoon appeared showing a Scotsman in full regalia in jail complaining, 'I failed the Tebbitt cricket test.'

The main reason why this is an issue of growing concern, as revealed by Tebbitt's remark, is of course immigration. But there are others that feed into it. One is the decline of the British Empire, another is devolution, with the existence now of a Scottish Parliament and a Welsh Assembly. These factors alone raise two questions. One is: what is it now to be English? The other is: what is it to be British? Further reasons why questions of identity are now very much on the agenda include the debate over regionalisation, membership of the European Union, the growing importance of religion as a marker of identity, and a general weakening of our national institutions, from the Sovereign and Parliament down to the local church.

Issues of identity are important in themselves. But I have a particular concern, and that is how a Christian perspective might make a difference to the way we understand and value them. Before anything else, though, it is important to try to make some clear distinctions between different kinds of identity, because this is a confusing, disputed area.

First, there are racial identities and ethnic identities, which can overlap but need not do so. We say someone is African or Asian or Caucasian. Such identities do not in themselves make for a political identity unless a particular government wishes to make it so – for example, the Nazis tried to make Germany an exclusively Aryan state, and in the modern world we have the terrible phenomenon of ethnic cleansing, which aims to create a political unit composed of people of identical ethnicity.

Secondly, there is national identity. A nation is a people with a common language and culture and a shared historical narrative. The people who belong to it are conscious of belonging together as a community over a period of time, but they may or may not form a state or even a political community. The Welsh and the Scots form nations and they now have a form of political expression through the Scottish Parliament and the Welsh Assembly, but they are part of a wider, British state. The Palestinians are a nation, and they have a form of political expression, but as of now they have no state of their own. The Kurds regard themselves as a nation, but they are split between different states.

The concept of the nation state belongs primarily to the period in Europe from the Reformation until the twentieth century, when there were many attempts to create culturally and religiously homogenous political units under different sovereigns. Before that period European unity, in so far as it existed, was built around the Papacy. With the Reformation, states sought their own centre of unity round the sovereign. This was always fraught with the potential for conflict, as the history of Europe shows. The origin of the terrible First World War is often attributed to the growing nationalism at the end of the nineteenth century, so now nationalism is usually regarded with deep suspicion. With nationalism in Europe there went along the concept of patriotism, and after the war there was a reaction against both nationalism and patriotism, as expressed, for example, in the poems of Wilfred Owen or the remark of E. M. Forster, who said:

> If I had to choose between betraying my country and betraying my friend I hope I would have the guts to betray my country.

Whilst we are right to be very wary of the concept of nationalism, and its associated idea of patriotism, which Dr Johnson termed 'the last refuge of the scoundrel', there are several reasons why we should not simply turn from it to a bland internationalism. One is that loves that are real and strong begin with the local, with our parents and family, and then outwards to the communities of which we are a part, and then out to include humanity as a whole. So a poet like Blake emphasised the importance of the particular rather than the general or abstract. Love of the local can and should grow into a love of the wider realm. A love of the wider realm that is not also rooted in the love of the local, can become abstract and unreal.

Then, as the Russian theologians tend to emphasise, nations are a special part of God's purpose. As Alexander Solzhenitsyn put it:

> Nations are the wealth of mankind, its collective personalities; the very least of them wears its own special colours and bears within itself a special face of divine intention.

That kind of view has its own great dangers; nevertheless we might say that individuals in their personal identity take on something of the special colour of the nation of which they are a part. They are in part shaped and nurtured by a national community which is 'a special face of the divine intention'.

Another reason is a more practical one, and related to our own time, with its intense drive towards globalisation. Globalisation erodes the traditional power of the nation state, because capital can be moved swiftly from one part of the world to another. A number of trans-national corporations are bigger than all but the largest states. This means that if the world, particularly in its economic realm, is to be ordered for the common good, the nation state needs to be strengthened – not on its own, but in regional and global alliances. Unless there are these groupings to strengthen the power of individual states in alliance with other states, the juggernaut of capitalism will carry all before it.

That said, there is a fundamental paradox about love of one's country. As Reinhold Niebuhr put it:

> There is an ethical paradox in patriotism which defies every but the most astute and sophisticated analysis. The paradox is that patriotism commutes individual unselfishness into national egoism ... so the Nation is at one and the same time a check upon, and a final vent for, the expression of individual egoism.[1]

To these identities, racial, ethnic and national, we might add cultural identity and religious identity. So people now talk of Britain as a multicultural society or a multi-faith one, meaning that the population now contains significant communities of people of differing cultural and religious backgrounds, though our public institutions in fact remain still predominantly Christian.

One of the advances in recent years has been the realisation that it is entirely right and proper for us to have multiple identities. In fact there is nothing new about this. St Paul defined himself as religiously a Jew. He lived in Tarsus in what is now south-east Turkey, and like everyone at that time, he would have had a strong sense of identification with his city, which was much stronger then than now, and Paul was proud of being 'a citizen of no mean city', as he put it. The Judaism in Tarsus, Hellenistic Judaism, was culturally very Greek. So Paul would have received a Greek, as well as a Hebrew education and he wrote his letters in the *koiné* or common Greek that was spoken all over the eastern Mediterranean. But if his culture was Greek, he also claimed proudly that he was a Roman citizen, and this entitled him to certain legal privileges, not least in his case, the right to appeal to Rome. So Paul had multiple, overlapping identities, and so do most of us if we think of it. I define myself as nationally Welsh, a British citizen, religiously Christian and culturally European.

RELIGION AS A MARKER OF IDENTITY

I now want to look in a little more detail at some of the pressures in our time that make this an issue of such importance. First, the issue of religion. What has happened and is still happening is that globalisation is making religion a marker of identity. We see this most clearly in countries like Indonesia, where people have moved from their traditional island or village communities into big cities to make goods for the Western market. In the village they had an identity as part of a traditionally ordered way of life. In the city, no such identity is available, and in gravitating to the mosque or church they find their identity as part of that religious community. There is nothing sinister about this in itself. Precisely the same occurs to British ex-pats living in Spain or the South of France. In Britain they may not have been great church-goers, but abroad they very often gravitate to one of the culturally English communities there, which may be the church – or for other people it might be the golf club. But of course in certain countries this situation can be exploited by extremists who want to stir up trouble, as in fact has happened in Indonesia in recent years. Indonesia was traditionally one of the most tolerant of Islamic countries but in recent years there have been some very ugly clashes between extreme Muslims and Christians. In Europe a related phenomenon was present in the break-up of the former Yugoslavia. This was a country on the border of Eastern and Western Christianity, so Serbia was Orthodox, but Croatia was Catholic. At the same time it was for a long time part of the Ottoman Empire, so there was a significant Muslim population in Bosnia and Kosovo. The wars there were certainly not caused by religion, but from time to time a war leader would play the religious card – because that was a way of getting the adherence of the community to which he belonged and which he wished to make militant.

In this country, again, there is a related phenomenon. Immigration has brought to our shores many people of non-Christian religions. Feeling lost in a new country, as we all do, it is natural to gather together around a mosque or temple, and the role of religion as a marker of identity is heightened. This obviously has important implications for how we go about trying to create a society in which people of different cultural and religious backgrounds feel fully included. In short, it is not enough simply to take into account their ethnic origin, which may be Pakistani, or Indian or whatever, because this might have become less important to them than the fact that they are Muslim or Sikh or Hindu.

I now want to look at racial and ethnic identity from a Christian point of view. They are not of course quite the same, but for my purposes now I can treat them in the same way because for each of us they are a given, a fact about us that we cannot change. John Sentamu, the Archbishop of York, feels strongly that there is only one race, the human race, and that is the only meaning we should give to the word 'race'. It is easy to understand and sympathise with why he says this, because the concept of race has been too often used to exclude and oppress particular groups of people. However, there are a couple of points that suggest that a more flexible use of the word might be in order. One is that it has sometimes been important for people to affirm their race or some other aspect of their identity as part of a process of affirming their worth after a period of subjugation. A good example of this occurred in recent history in America, where the slogan 'Black is beautiful' was embraced by Black Americans. Another related example is the gay pride marches in different parts of the world. People want to join with others in affirming an aspect of their identity that had previously been rejected in some way. This is obviously very different from a particular racial group in a position of power, asserting that power to exclude or oppress those of other, weaker racial groups.

Then, the fact that certain things about us are a given is, from a Christian point of view, an aspect of the doctrine of creation. God has created us as part of the world in all its aspects, not as wispy spirits or disembodied souls. We are embodied, and we are embodied as particular persons. I am born at a particular time of history, of a particular ethnic origin, in a particular cultural grouping. This is all part of the creation about which God in the book of Genesis says, 'And behold, it was very good.' Of course, many of us regard ourselves as cosmopolitan, or internationalist in outlook, and we claim to sit light to ethnic or national differences. But the fact is that these are part of what makes me me, and you you. As mentioned earlier, we are more likely to love wider humanity if we have first a proper love of ourselves and the local communities of which we are a part.

One crucial fact, of which we are probably more consciously aware than our forebears, is that identity is to a significant degree a human construct. Clearly, some things about us and the wider social and national groupings to which we belong are a given. It is a fact that I was born on a particular day in a particular city. It is a fact that I am white, getting on in years and male. There are some grey areas even here, of course. Some people find themselves born with a body that is physiologically of one sex, but emotionally and spiritually they feel, from an early age, that they really belong to the other one. So we have a certain number of trans-gendered people. Then there is the question of our sexuality, which is also important to our identity. Some people think that sexual orientation can be changed. Personally I believe that for the vast majority of people, this is neither possible nor appropriate. Some people, particularly in their early years, may be uncertain about their sexuality. Most gay people did not choose to be gay, but discovered that they were gay. For them, their sexuality is a given fact about their identity.

But leaving aside a few disputed areas, we can say there are facts about our identity that are a given. At the same time, there are other things about us which are much more open to how we might want to understand and define ourselves. I like to describe myself as Welsh. My mother's side are English, so I could equally well have chosen to describe myself as English. For a variety of reasons, I like to think of myself and describe myself as Welsh. This is a construct. It could have been different.

At a personal level, this kind of issue can be fun – at a national level it is of huge social significance. For example, historians now argue that British identity, far from being something that has been fixed and final down the ages, was in very large measure a creation of the eighteenth century, and was obviously linked to imperialism and the concept of British superiority. The year 1707, which saw the formation of the United Kingdom of Britain and Ireland (which later became the United Kingdom of Britain and Northern Ireland), is regarded as the key date. Then, as Linda Colley has put it, Britain was an invented nation:

> Heavily dependent for its raison d'etre on a broadly
> protestant culture, on the threat and tonic of recurrent war,
> especially war with France, and on the triumphs, profits, and
> 'otherness' represented by a massive overseas empire.

Over the last two decades a good debate has been going on about British identity today, with all kinds of suggestions from political leaders, academic and government reports, thinktanks and newspapers. In what does it or ought it to consist? If there is a lack of British identity today, how should we go about reconstructing it? One aspect of this has to do with multiculturalism. Recently there has been a reaction against the emphasis on multiculturalism which has been an assumed basis of policy for the last 30 or 40 years. Some are worried that the reaction against this may go too far, and may fail to take into account the fact that we are in fact a multicultural society, composed of people whose views will need to be taken into account if they are to feel any sense of identification with the nation of which they are citizens. Tariq Modood, who writes about these issues with knowledge and good sense, thinks that we do indeed need a civic rebalancing, but not an end to multiculturalism as such. He is suspicious about taking a set of values, like equality, liberty, enterprise and so on, as he thinks these are either platitudinous or too disputed to be of use, and that, as he puts it, 'National identity should be woven in debate and discussion, not reduced to a list.'

That is fair, but of course the discussion has to begin somewhere, and where it should begin is with what our history and culture have given us. It is at this point that mention must be made of religious forms of dress like the *burkah* and the *niquab*. As indicated earlier, religion has become an important marker of identity, which is why this cannot simply be a matter of public indifference. A view has to be taken. This has of course been done by President Sarkozy, who wants Islamic religious dress banned in France. In Turkey, in principle a strongly secular state, but one in which Islam is very important, the issue of headscarves continues to be highly controversial. This is not an issue that can be considered as though every state was the same. What I would want to say about the British situation, is that they should be allowed in the same way that the Sikh turban is allowed and is now familiar. Like many others, I find the *burkah* and, to a lesser extent, the *niquab* unsettling. I don't like it. But whether I like it or not, is not the point. A state that seeks to be inclusive of a variety of cultures, where culture and religion are sometimes closely bound up, will respect people's desire to symbolise their faith in this particular way. But every society is different, and I do not think that this kind of attitude is necessarily the correct one for every other country in the world at this particular stage in history.

BRITISH IDENTITY

America, as we know, despite its hugely varied ethnic makeup, has a strong sense of national identity symbolised by the flag, and standing to attention before it with one arm across the chest, on big occasions. It has been suggested that in this country we need to find something equivalent in order to generate a sense of British solidarity and loyalty across all our various communities. I am a little sceptical about such ideas myself, for I suspect that symbolic expressions of loyalty have to grow naturally and organically, and any attempt to impose something like that would strike people as artificial. However, the concept of Britishness has two components – what we might call the emotional pull, and the values enshrined in the idea of British citizenship. The latter is of great importance, and needs serious attention. It is right that people who have newly acquired British citizenship should take part in a citizenship ceremony, and I understand that these have turned out to be something of a success. It is right that children should be

---

taught citizenship at school, and that this should be an important and not a marginal part of the curriculum. Children are also taught history at school, and what is taught in that class clearly has a very close relationship to the pupil's understanding of who they are and their identity as citizens. So first something about this.

History in the old days was very much a national narrative about kings and queens, great men and the advance of empire. It is, I suspect, taught very differently now. From a Christian point of view, it seems to me that the key principle we will want to bring to bear, not alone but along with other concerns, will be one of inclusivity. The key characteristic of the ministry and teaching of Jesus was his desire to include those whom others excluded. This has implications for all aspects of life, personal and political. It means that the national narrative taught in schools will be such as to make all the pupils in the class feel that they belong to this society about whom they are being taught. So it will not just be about men, but about women; not just about movers and shakers, but the vast majority of humanity, the nameless poor. It will not just be history from the standpoint of the imperialist, but from that of the subjugated; so it will not just be a history of white people, but of Asian and Black people and of their contributions both to civilisation in general and to the history of this country in particular. There should be a national narrative – for there will be one, whether people think there is or not – and therefore the one we have should be done consciously. It should in effect be constructed with a view to what we want to achieve through it. A good example in recent years has been the way people have started to think of immigration, particularly in relation to the East End – not as something that began after World War II but as a feature of our history for two thousand years, and not as a threat but as an enrichment. An attempt was made to do this on the stage recently with a play at the National Theatre entitled *English people very nice*. Of course, it is possible to go to the opposite extreme and seek to create a national narrative like that in the Soviet Union, Fascist Germany and nationalist dictatorships the world over. So we need to be on our guard here. National narratives are indeed constructs, but they have to be rooted in the truth, and this means dealing with the dark side, the negativities of national history, as well as its achievements. It is not a question of fabrication but of selection, ordering and emphasis within the totality of what is available to pass on from the past to the next generation. It was very good to read not long ago that Germany and France have now published a joint history for teaching in schools. It is wonderful to think how much chauvinistic damage a history like that can undo just through the facts it selects and how it puts them forward.

This national narrative can clearly play its part in bringing about a healthy emotional attachment to the idea of being British. Depending on what is taught and how it is taught, pupils will be found to belong and define themselves in that way, or they will be alienated. But, as I have suggested, though important, this emotional content has to grow naturally and organically. At the same time as this creative teaching of history through an inclusive national narrative, there is the important question of what people can and should commit themselves to when they describe themselves as British citizens. Those who acquire British citizenship are currently supposed to swear:

> I, (*name*), swear by Almighty God that on becoming a British citizen I will be faithful and bear true allegiance to Her Majesty Queen Elizabeth, her heirs and successors according to law.
>
> I will give my loyalty to the United Kingdom and respect its rights and freedoms. I will uphold its democratic values. I will observe its laws faithfully and fulfil my duties and obligations as a British citizen.

Timothy Garton Ash says about the first part of this oath:

> Now I myself am rather attached to the novels of Sir Walter Scott, but in 2008 this is an amazing load of anachronistic bunkum. First of all, let's leave God out of it, shall we? Secondly what on earth does it mean to 'bear true allegiance' to Her Majesty, and why should I extend this courtesy to Prince William, let alone Harry?[2]

Perhaps the language is unnecessarily anachronistic, but that does not mean to say that the sentiments themselves can simply be thrown away. As a teenager, I was a republican. In those days the national anthem was played at the end of every public performance in the theatre and cinema. When my mother stood to attention, I remained firmly in my seat and a fierce row ensued. It was some years later that I was converted from this view – by a casual conversation. I was attending some official gathering at Westfield College, in the University of London, and chatting to Norman St John Stevas, as he then was (now he is Lord St John of Fawsley). Somehow we got onto the question of the Monarch, and he pointed out that the Sovereign was the one symbol we now have that in some way unites the whole of our society. He was right, and despite the decline in the prestige of the monarchy since then, and active hostility to it in some quarters, it is still about the only symbol we have. Furthermore, the basis of our constitution, though unwritten, is not simply Parliament, but the Queen in Parliament under God. When there is so little that binds our country together, it seems foolish to jettison what, for all its historic faults, has in fact been a central feature in our national identity for hundreds of years, if not longer. Edmund Burke's understanding of society as something organic, persisting over time, with obligations both to the past and the future, always changing but doing so incrementally, rather than by a violent chopping away, seems relevant here.

With the second part of the oath of allegiance, Timothy Garton Ash firmly agrees, and so do I. This encapsulates the essentials of what it means to be a British citizen, with the emphasis on citizenship. As I have suggested earlier, the emotional content of this, its symbolic expression and so on, probably has to grow organically and naturally. An example of such growth in relation to Englishness, rather than being British, is the emergence of flags of St George in recent years, not least at sporting fixtures, rather than the Union Jack.

Citizenship is a different matter. This is a concern which the Government has a proper responsibility to promote, and which it now seeks to do in various ways, as already mentioned. It should certainly include education about the rights and responsibilities of citizenship, teaching about the rule of law and the political values underlying it, and about our system of parliamentary democracy. None of this, perhaps, is very sexy, but it is essential if our society is to be a value-based one, in which people participate and to which they feel a real sense of belonging, whatever ethnic or religious background they come from.

CITIZENS OF HEAVEN

From a Christian point of view this emphasis on citizenship is firmly rooted in the New Testament and carried forward in all mainstream theology, Catholic and Protestant. Of course, in the New Testament we have a very different political system – an empire with little corresponding to our liberal democracies. This was an empire that was in many ways hostile to the newly emerging Christian Church – there was a fierce period of persecution under Nero in 66, for example, which is reflected in the pages of the New Testament. But despite this, the New Testament still stressed the importance of government. There is a famous passage in St Paul's letter to the Romans where he tells his readers that we are to obey the secular authorities. He says this is

> an obligation imposed not merely by fear of retribution
> but by conscience. This is also why you pay taxes. The
> authorities are in God's service and it is to this they devote
> their energies.

> Romans 13:5–6

In subsequent Church history and theology, it is the teaching and example of St Augustine that sets the pattern. According to him, as outlined in his major work, *The City of God*, Christians are members of the City of God, which God is building up through human history. But at the same time, in this life we are members of the earthly city, and here it is our duty to work with people of good will for the peace, order and justice without which no human society can exist. So Augustine himself, as mentioned earlier, as well as being a bishop, spent a great deal of time as a magistrate. Indeed, one of the ways in which the Church consolidated its position in the fourth century was by bishops taking over positions in city councils that had previously been occupied by secular magistrates. So the concept of being a good citizen is very firmly rooted in both the New Testament and subsequent Christian teaching. Christians thought of themselves as first and foremost citizens of heaven, but this reinforced their desire to be good citizens of the earthly cities to which they belonged.

IDENTITY IN FLUX

Now I want to go back to an earlier crucial point about all identities being to a significant degree a human construct. In short, identities have changed, are changing and will continue to change in the future. There is nothing fixed and final about who we are. Let me consider this at a personal level. This is brought out in a very moving poem by Dietrich Bonhoeffer. Bonhoeffer, you may remember, was a distinguished theologian in the 1930s who, in reaction to Hitler's policy of 'Aryanising' the Church – that is, eliminating all Jewish elements from it – was one of the founders of the Confessing Church, and indeed, he ran their seminary. He took part in the plot to assassinate Hitler, was imprisoned and shot shortly before the end of the war. Whilst in prison he wrote letters, prayers and poems, subsequently published in *Letters and Papers from Prison* which made a major impact in the 1960s. One of the poems is called 'Who am I?'

> Who am I? They often tell me
> I stepped from my cell's confinement
> Calmly, cheerfully, firmly,
> Like a squire from his country house ...
> Am I then really all that which other men tell of?
> Or am I only what I myself know of myself?
> Restless and longing and sick like a bird in a cage ...
> Who am I? This or the other?

Am I one person today and to-morrow another?
Am I both at once? A hypocrite before others,
And before myself a contemptibly woebegone weakling? ...
Who am I? They mock me, these lonely questions of mine.
Whoever I am, Thou knowest, O God, I am thine!

I very much like the double meaning of that last line.

We may not know who we are, but God does. Then, whoever we are, we belong to him. In the future, when his future for us is accomplished, we will be who we truly are.

This is a point powerfully made in the first letter of John:

> Dear friends, we are now God's children; what we shall be has not yet been disclosed, but we know that when Christ appears we shall be like him, because we shall see him as he is.

1 John 3:2

In other words, again, our true identity will be fully revealed and known only in the future. For we are made in the image of God, and called to grow into his likeness, the likeness that shines in the face of Christ. This identity in Christ does not take away from our distinctiveness, but brings it to its true fulfilment.

This is to put it in personal terms. But our personal identity is inseparable from our membership of various communities, from the family to the state. The same principle holds there. National identity, like religious identity, is in a constant state of change. It is in part a given, but even more significantly, it has still to be created. As one Anglican report has commented:

> Christian loyalty is a commitment to a nation conceived as being itself a process – of sharing, struggling and change; a commitment to what might be rather than simply what has been ... Loyalty is the decision to be actively part of such a process.[3]

TOWARDS A CHRISTIAN UNDERSTANDING OF THE COMMON GOOD[4]

I suggested in the Introduction to this book that there are some signs of a shift in the tectonic plates of the underlying philosophy of our society. The time has come to indicate the implications of this, taking up some of the threads in the previous chapters.[5]

Since the nineteenth century one of the dominant approaches to political philosophy has been utilitarianism, the idea that we should try to produce the greatest happiness for the greatest number. This philosophy has been of great benefit in helping to bring about progressive social change, and it will remain valuable for many issues of social policy. However, its weaknesses were apparent from the first. One is that different kinds of happiness or different kinds of pleasure cannot be weighed on the same scale. There are qualitative, not just quantitative differences between different kinds of pleasure. The other difficulty is that it cannot do justice to our gut instinct that certain things are just wrong, try to justify them as we may. The most obvious contemporary example is torture. Most people would say that whatever arguments you put forward to justify torture, such as saving the lives of innocent people, it is still wrong. It is this set of moral convictions, rooted in a sense of the worth of every single individual, that undergirds all talk about human rights.

The other dominant philosophy, which takes two forms, is liberalism, which emphasises the priority of personal choice. Economic liberalism applies this to the market and says, let the market rule supreme. Leave people free to consume and produce what they want. This view is unhistorical, in that Adam Smith, the intellectual fount of the market economy, was quite clear that the markets needed to be rooted in certain moral principles, and its best defenders in recent years have tried to say the same, without getting much response in practice. Michael Sandel draws attention to what happened in New Orleans after the terrible flooding there. Some people tried to exploit the situation by selling basic goods at truly exorbitant prices. An unqualified admirer of the free market devoid of moral values would support this. People were so

---

desperate that they were prepared to pay 100 times the normal value of goods, and there were people ready to sell them for that price. What utilitarianism does not take into account is the widespread sense of outrage in America that people's desperate need should have been exploited in this way. It was felt to be wrong: honourable people in an honourable society did not do this kind of thing. In short, moral judgements and values came into play. More widely, many people would feel that there are certain areas where the market should not rule. It would be wrong to have a free market in organs, for example. It would be wrong to sell places at university to those who would pay the highest price for them.

The other form of liberalism is social liberalism. This says that people should be free to choose their own lifestyle, and they should not have one imposed on them by society as a whole. It is easy to see why this view has been so popular. One reason is that there is widespread disagreement over lifestyles. The other is a fear that if we start talking about virtue as a value that the whole community should exhibit, there will arise an oppressive moralism. This was perhaps the fear that stopped the movement known as communitarianism making more headway a few years ago. But can we avoid making judgements about virtue and value? In an earlier chapter on law and morality I mentioned my own feeling as a member of the Home Office Advisory Committee for the Reform of the Law on Sexual Offences when we considered offences against animals. I realised I had a deep conviction that certain forms of behaviour were incompatible with what it means to be a human being. Michael Sandel gives another example. A man in Germany advertised for someone who would be willing to be killed and eaten; 200 people answered the advert, and four were interviewed. One person was killed, cooked and eaten. German law could not convict the person of murder, for it was totally consensual, though they did find another way of convicting and imprisoning the man. But whatever the law says, most people would find such an action deeply abhorrent and something which society should not allow, however consensual. Again, issues of value emerge, not just for the individual, but for the kind of society which we want.

When we begin to reflect on the kind of society we want, then we cannot avoid asking the question about what society is for. The same question is raised in relation to every institution. What is a university for? What is a school for? Until you answer that question you cannot begin to think about what it is that the institution should value, and indeed on what basis people should be allowed to enter it. We are in fact back with Aristotle, who taught that we must decide on the purpose of something before we can decide what is good. The good is what fits the purpose. If a university exists to foster intellectual excellence, then this is what it will honour, and it is on this basis that people will be allowed to enter.

At this point we also need to reflect a little about the nature of the choices we make, and what makes a choice a moral choice. Kant, who has been so influential in the modern world, said that a choice is only moral if it is done out of a sense of duty. He suggested two basic principles to guide us. One is that we must act in such a way that everyone could act in that way in similar circumstances. We must be able to universalise what we choose. Secondly, we should treat other human beings as ends in themselves, not as a means to an end. He thought that only when we did this as a matter of duty were we really free, and only then was it a truly moral act. If we wanted to do it, or liked doing it, this was not relevant to its moral dimension. Kant is important in forcing us to be morally consistent, with his test of universalisability, and his emphasis on human beings as ends in themselves. However, there is something very odd about his understanding of what makes an action moral. Most people would say that they would like others to value them because they wanted to do so, not just out of a sense of duty. It puts someone who warmly and spontaneously loves their husband or wife in an odd position. They love them with their whole being, but on a strict understanding of Kant, this does not count as a moral act. Now a sense of duty is certainly both vital and neglected today, but it has to do with being consistent with our responsibilities whether or not we feel like it. It surely cannot mean that when we do feel like doing what is also our duty, the action is morally insignificant.

Kant was a Christian, but from the standpoint of Christian theology he has really relapsed into a false mind/body dualism. In making an abyss between feelings and duty he is not being true to the Christian understanding of human beings as embodied. Ordinary human experience suggests that we want the virtues we admire – say courage, or generosity – to become part of us. Of course, for most of the time we have to try to emulate people who show those virtues, and we have to try to act them out, even if we do not feel them. But we hope for a time when, through the grace of God, they will become part of our very being.

This again takes us back to the kind of choices we make. The hugely influential modern philosopher Alastair MacIntyre argued that we do not make our choices in a vacuum, but as part of a moral tradition. We are born and shaped by a moral tradition, and until we opt for another one, we make our choices within the parameters it provides. This moral tradition will be inseparable from a particular understanding of what it means to be a human being. Or to put it another way, we find ourselves part of a communal story, a story which has a particular understanding of the goal and purpose of human life. The choices we make when young are shaped by the tradition we have been brought up in. So our freedom is not a naked one, shorn of all that is distinctive about me as a citizen of a particular country and a member of a particular religion at a particular time; it is a choice to be made within that continuum. We are not only embodied as individuals, we are embodied in communities, and these help to give us our identity. So for Christians, our choices are made within the body of Christ, within the community of Christians, shaped by the past and looking to the future, including a future beyond space and time.

For all these reasons it means that a theory of government based on a hypothetical contract, whether put forward by Hobbes, Locke or Rawls, is inadequate by itself. The view of Rawls is important as a benchmark for fairness and a challenge to all our ideas of justice, as discussed in the section on equality in Chapter 3, but it falsely assumes a naked choice shorn of all personal loyalties. For most human beings, there are particular loyalties, to their own children or parents, their city or team, their country. This can be questioned, and it may not always be right to accord these particular, personal loyalties priority over an obligation to the wider community or wider world. However, as we are born and grow up, we experience the moral claim of these loyalties, and they have to be taken into account in the choices we make. They are part of the story which shaped us, and which we in turn are shaping by the choices we make. Our children and children's children will be born into and shaped by this story in their turn.

Against the background of these considerations, what kind of society should a Christian desire? Of course there will always be disagreements about the nature of that good, but as Michael Sandel has written:

> To achieve a just society we have to reason together about the meaning of the good life, and to create a public culture hospitable to the disagreements that will inevitably arise.[6]

We have to reason together. That was also the conclusion of Amartya Sen in his discussion mentioned earlier in the book. He suggested that a case can be made out for each of the dominant political philosophies of our time. No one can totally exclude the validity of the other perspectives. So in any situation we have to make a judgement. Furthermore, a good society is not one in which a particular political philosophy reigns supreme. A good society is one in which we take all voices and the needs they represent into account. In a globalised world this means taking marginalised voices from outside our borders into account in our national deliberations. He looks to the parable of the Good Samaritan as a model for taking the outsider into consideration and not drawing the definition of our neighbour in narrow terms. Like Sandel, the essence of democracy for Sen is reasoning together, taking into account the key values of liberty and equality, but doing so in relation to the actual practical outcomes of different societies, not imposing an abstract philosophical blueprint.

Earlier in this book I quoted T. S. Eliot who described the society he wanted in these words:

> It would be a society in which the natural end of man – virtue and well-being in community – is acknowledged for all, and the supernatural end – beatitude – for those who have the eyes to see it.[7]

This is a very appealing description which I could certainly live with. Nevertheless, I think it needs to be put somewhat differently today. First, the phrase 'virtue and well-being' does not reflect the emphasis on growth and development which we now regard as desirable. Secondly, the world 'virtue' has for many people too moralistic a tone to it, as well as being focused on morality, whereas in the modern world we are concerned with the development of the whole person – body, mind and spirit – as a unity. So instead of 'virtue and well-being' I would prefer 'the development of gifts and character'. Then, thirdly, the phrase 'in community', though welcome, does not quite do justice to the essentially polar nature of person and community. It is not just that persons live in community; without human community, there could be no persons. Furthermore communities, like persons, have qualities and character and are open to change and development. They need to be seen together. So although I cannot devise as felicitous a sentence as Eliot's, the first half of my understanding of a desirable society would be:

> A society in which the natural end of human beings – personal and communal development of gifts and character – is acknowledged for all.

What about the last half of Eliot's statement: 'the supernatural end – beatitude – for those who have eyes to see it'? The contrast between the two halves of the sentence, between what is acknowledged for all and what is there for those with eyes to see it, is one with which I am in sympathy. It reflects the conviction of traditional natural law theory, that there are morally desirable states and qualities which all can see and to which all are called to respond, whether someone is a religious believer or not. We can see the force of this by thinking about any good school we know. Such a school will seek to have an ethos in which there is mutual respect, a concern for others both within the school and outside. It will be inclusive in the sense that it will want every pupil to develop their particular potential and talents. All schools will have some such ideal, however they might be failing at any one moment, and whether or not they are faith schools. Furthermore, parents who send children to schools will want the school to have some such ideal. In short, this is a natural ideal, whether it is for a school or society as a whole.

On Eliot's formula, the religious dimension is in no way imposed. It is simply there, as part of the history and culture for those with eyes to see it. Nevertheless, the word 'beatitude' needs a little unpacking. It could just convey the idea of an individual soul's relationship with God. In fact, as the collect for All Saints' Day puts it, we are 'knit together in one communion and fellowship in the mystical body' of Christ. We come before God, now and in eternity, as members of the body of Christ. This body, like earthly human communities, is open to growth and development, not just of gifts and character, but in the knowledge and love of God. Or to put it another way, we have been made in the image of God, but we are called, within the mystical body, to grow into the divine likeness. This is what is meant by 'beatitude'.

Like Aristotle, Christians begin not with the question about what is right, but what is the good. For us, God is good, all good, our true and everlasting good. The end or goal of human life is to grow into that likeness, not as solitary individuals, but within the mystical body of Christ. Whilst we are on this earth, there is a counterpart to this in our human communities of all kinds, including both civil society and the body politic. As I formulated it above:

> It would be a society in which the natural end of human beings – personal and communal development of gifts and character – is acknowledged for all.

This is an understanding of the common good which I believe we should try to build into our life together, allowing it to shape that life, whether it is at a local, national or international level. It is in and through the process of doing this that we find our individual identity.

NOTES

INTRODUCTION

1. It is said that Alec Douglas-Home's mother once remarked, 'I think it is *so* good of Alec to do Prime Minister.'
2. Anthony Seldon, *Trust* (Biteback Publishing, 2009), p. 71.
3. T. S. Eliot, *The Idea of a Christian Society* (Faber and Faber, 1982), p. 82.
4. A sentence often attributed to Winston Churchill, but it may in fact come from Reinhold Niebuhr.

Chapter 1: SPEAKING FOR GOD IN A SECULAR AGE

1. A. J. P. Taylor, *English History 1914–1945* (OUP, 1965), p. 1.
2. A point made by Edward Norman, a scholar very critical of church pronouncements on public affairs. Though highly critical, for the reason given above, he argued, 'In the world the Christian seeks to apply the great love of God as well as he can in contemporary terms. And that will actually involve corporate social and political action.' Edward Norman, *Christianity and World Order* (OUP, 1965), p. 79.
3. Charles Taylor, *A Secular Age* (Harvard University Press, 2007).
4. Amartya Sen, *The Argumentative Indian* (Allen Lane, 2005).
5. Ronald Dworkin, *Is Democracy Possible Here?* (Princeton, 2006).
6. I became aware of this when, as a member of the Royal Commission on the Reform of the House of Lords (the Wakenham Commission), we received a delegation from the churches of Britain and Northern Ireland. I was conscious of 'ancestral voices' – the historic, and as it turned out, continuing resentment of the non-Anglican churches about the privileged position of the Church of England.
7. These are the questions behind *Religious Voices in Public Places*, ed. Nigel Biggar and Linda Hogan (OUP, 2009). There is a particularly thorough analysis of the position of John Rawls in the chapter by Raymond Plant.
8. Ibid., p. 34.
9. Jonathan Chaplin, *Talking God: The Legitimacy of Religious Public Reasoning* (Theos, 2008). Working with the distinction between programmatic and procedural secularism, he makes the important point that the latter is not always as neutral as its advocates suggest. Assumptions can be smuggled into

even procedural issues, as on the issue of the funding of political parties, for here it is a question of whether economic or political freedom is given the greater weight. One of the ways in which an illegitimate assumption has got into the debate on procedural secularism is the view that the only kind of public reasoning that is acceptable is one that does not overtly refer to a religious basis for it. If a religiously based reason is put forward, it is apparently felt by some people that this is a failure of respect, for equality of respect demands that all reasons be equally accessible. Chaplin rightly says that what matters is equality of persons, and in fact this does not just allow but demands confessional candour on behalf of the religious and non-religious alike. Whether religiously based reasons are put forward will depend very much on the context, and it may be right to be very sparing, but they cannot be ruled out in principle. Furthermore, religiously based reasons will often go alongside reasons that do not have that basis, the one spelling out or reinforcing the other.

10. He continues to be influential and has made a major impact – for example, on the outlook of President Obama. See *Reinhold Niebuhr and Contemporary Politics: God and Power*, ed. Richard Harries and Stephen Platten (OUP, 2009).

11. See Richard Harries, *The Re-enchantment of Christian Morality* (SPCK, 2008).

12. Two of the best known are Stanley Hauerwas and John Milbank. Their influence has been shown in, for example, Samuel Wells and Ben Quash. See *Reinhold Niebuhr and Contemporary Politics*, ed. Richard Harries and Stephen Platten (OUP, 2010), where this approach is contrasted with the very different one of Reinhold Niebuhr.

13. Ronald J. Sider and Richard K. Taylor, *Nuclear Holocaust and Christian Hope* (Hodder and Stoughton, 1983), p. 132.

14. Oliver O'Donovan has organised his political theology around the theme of judgement. But our expectations of government cannot be kept within that category today, however widely O'Donovan interprets the nature of judgement. See his *The Ways of Judgment* (Eerdmans, 2005).

15. On a rough calculation it is well over 5000 words. *Theology* asks that essays submitted be not longer than 3500 words.

16. Fisher Papers, Vol. 171, pp. 309ff.

17. Paul Ramsey, *Who Speaks for the Church?* (St Andrews Press, 1969).

18. Ibid., p. 247.

19. Ramsey Papers, Vol. 105, p. 271. Lord Saltoun was going to make a speech in the House of Lords critical of Ramsey, and wrote to him to make sure he quoted him accurately.

20. Ramsey Papers, Vol. 85, p. 311.

Chapter 2: LAW AND MORALITY

1. Boethius, *The Consolation of Philosophy*, VIII (Loeb Classical Library, 1973), p. 227.

2. See Richard Harries, *The Re-enchantment of Morality* (SPCK, 2008).

3. Karl Marx, *The Poverty of Philosophy*.

4. Basil Mitchell, *Law, Morality and Religion in a Secular Society* (OUP, 1967) p.120.

5. T. S. Eliot, *The Idea of a Christian Society and Other Writings* (Faber, 1982), p. 82.
6. As Amartya Sen rightly argues in *The Idea of Justice* (Allen Lane, 2009).

Chapter 3: WHAT MAKES US THINK GOD WANTS DEMOCRACY?

1. The *Observer*, 30 Sept. 2007, p. 9.
2. David Nicholls was especially alert to this danger. For he showed, particularly in *Deity and Domination* (Routledge, 1989), but also elsewhere, how easy it is for people to have a picture of God that reflects all too closely the political system of the time. As he put it in relation to the dominant image of God in our own time: 'Modern western Christians have indeed invented a God without enemies, a God who does not take sides, but spends his time conciliating and manipulating, like a celestial personnel manager. He is the God of the comfortable and contented ... The modern emphasis on welfare images of God must be judged as unbalanced – uncritically reflecting, as they do, the ideology of a welfare state' (pp. 242–3).
3. Some of this chapter also appears in *Reinhold Niebuhr and Contemporary Politics: God and Power*, ed. Richard Harries and Stephen Platten (OUP, 2010).
4. Reinhold Niebuhr, *The Children of Light and the Children of Darkness* (London, Nisbet, 1945), p. vi.
5. Richard Fox, *Reinhold Niebuhr, A Biography* (Pantheon, 1985), p. 220.
6. Niebuhr, *The Children of Light and the Children of Darkness*, op. cit., p. 91.
7. Ibid., p. 34.
8. Ibid., p. 99.
9. C. S. Lewis, 'Equality', reprinted in the Canadian *C. S. Lewis Journal*, Summer 1990. It originally appeared in *The Spectator* in 1943. See also his *A Preface to Paradise Lost* (OUP, 1942), chap. XI, where he is highly critical of the failure of modern critics to understand the proper role of hierarchy in Milton and other Western thinkers.
10. Oliver O'Donovan, *The Ways of Judgment* (Eerdmans, 2005), p. 168.
11. Ibid., p. 170.
12. Ibid., p. 173.
13. Ibid., p. 178.
14. John de Gruchy, 'Democracy' in *The Oxford Companion to Christian Thought*, ed. Adrian Hastings (OUP, 2000), p. 157. See also John de Gruchy, *Christianity and Democracy* (Cambridge University Press, 1995).
15. Amartya Sen, *The Idea of Justice* (Allen Lane, 2009).
16. T. S. Eliot, *The Idea of a Christian Society and Other Writings* (Faber, 1982), p. 48.
17. Ibid., p. 48.
18. A point made in a number of articles, quoted by Charles C. Brown, *Niebuhr and His Age: Reinhold Niebuhr's Prophetic Role in the Twentieth Century* (Trinity Press, 1992), p. 217.
19. 'Christianity and Crisis', 8 April 1947, reprinted in *Reinhold Niebuhr, Theologian of Public Life, Selected Writings*, ed. Larry Rasmussen (Collins, 1989), p. 256.
20. Ibid., p. 256.
21. Ibid., p. 100.

Chapter 4: LIBERTY, EQUALITY AND HUMAN COMMUNITY

1. Fyodor Dostoevsky, *The Brothers Karamazov*, trans. David Magarshak (Penguin, 1958), p. 301.
2. John Stuart Mill, *On Liberty* (Penguin, 1986), p. 67.
3. Graham Greene, *The Comedians* (Penguin, 1966), p. 283.
4. William Temple, *Christianity and the Social Order* (London, Penguin, 1946), p. 67.
5. This is one of the themes of Richard Harries, *The Re-enchantment of Morality* (SPCK, 2008).
6. Ronald Dworkin, 'Liberalism', in *Public and Private Morality*, ed. Stuart Hampshire (CUP, 1978), p. 131.
7. R. H. Tawney, *Equality* (Allen and Unwin, 1964), p. 106.
8. Amartya Sen, *The Idea of Justice* (Allen Lane, 2009).
9. Michael Sandel, *Justice: What's the Right Thing to Do?* (Allen Lane, 2009).
10. Simon Jenkins, *Guardian*, 4 Feb. 2009.
11. See Richard Harries, *Is There a Gospel for the Rich?* (Mowbray, 1992).
12. David Hare, *The Power of Yes* (Faber and Faber, 2009), pp. 75–6.

Chapter 5: DOES GOD BELIEVE IN HUMAN RIGHTS?

1. A point strongly and rightly emphasised by Amartya Sen, *The Idea of Justice* (Allen Lane, 2009), chap. 17.
2. This is discussed in Richard Harries, *The Re-enchantment of Morality* (SPCK, 2008).
3. Roger Rushton, 'Religious truths and human coexistence', *Does God Believe in Human Rights?*, ed. Nazila Ghanea, Alan Stephens and Raphael Walden (Leiden, Martinus Nijhoff, 2007), p. 42.
4. J. Mahoney, *The Challenge of Human Rights* (Blackwell, 2007).
5. D. H. Lawrence, *'Stand Up!', The Complete Poems*, ed. Vivian De Sola Pinto and Warrant Roberts (Heinemann, 1964), Vol. I, p. 560.
6. Ronald Dworkin, *Taking Rights Seriously* (Duckworth, 1978), p. 198.
7. Amartya Sen, 'Law and Human Rights', *The British Institute of Human Rights Brief*, Summer 2005, p. 12.
8. Frank McGuiness, *There Came a Gypsy Riding* (Faber, 2000), p. 75.
9. Margaret MacDonald, 'Natural Rights', *Theories of Rights*, ed. Jeremy Waldron (OUP, 1984), p. 37.
10. Ibid., p. 36.
11. Dworkin, *Taking Rights Seriously*, op. cit., p. xi.
12. Ronald Dworkin, *Guardian*, 24 May 2006, p. 28.
13. See John Nurser, *For All Peoples and All Nations* (Geneva, WCC Publications, 2005).
14. All the main documents relating to human rights are in Paul Sieghart, *The Lawful Rights of Mankind* (OUP, 1985).
15. José Miguez Bonino, 'Religious Commitment and Human Rights: A Christian Perspective', in *Understanding Human Rights: An Interdisciplinary and Integrated Study*, ed. Alan Falconer (Irish School of Ecumenics, 1980), p. 32.

16. Mahoney, *The Challenge of Human Rights*, op. cit., p. 64.

Chapter 6: WHO DO WE THINK WE ARE? NATIONAL AND RELIGIOUS IDENTITIES

1. Reinhold Niebuhr, *Moral Man and Immoral Society* (Charles Scribner's, 1932), pp. 91–3.
2. Timothy Garton Ash, *Guardian*, 13 March 2008.
3. *Peacemaking in a Nuclear Age*, Report of a Working Party of the Board for Social Responsibility of the Church of England (Church House Publishing, 1988), p. 47.
4. The concept of the common good has been an important one in Catholic social teaching in recent decades. See Clifford Longley, 'Government and the Common Good', in *God and Government* (SPCK, 2009), chap. 7.
5. This is very apparent in the books by Amartya Sen and Michael Sandel discussed here, but there has also been a counterpart to this in much recent writing from Christians, for example in the book *Religious Voices in Public Places*, discussed in Chapter 1, and in the good work being done by the Theos organisation through their booklets.
6. Michael Sandel, *Justice: What's the Right Thing to Do?* (Allen Lane, 2009), p. 261.
7. T. S. Eliot, *The Idea of a Christian Society* (Faber, 1982), p. 62.

INDEX